Talking Abou

Talking About Death

A Pastoral Guide

Susan Walker

CANTERBURY
PRESS
Norwich

Published in 2022 by Canterbury Press
Editorial office
3rd Floor, Invicta House,
108–114 Golden Lane,
London EC1Y 0TG, UK
www.canterburypress.co.uk

Canterbury Press is an imprint of Hymns Ancient & Modern Ltd
(a registered charity)

H
Y **Ancient**
M
N *&* **Modern**
S

Hymns Ancient & Modern® is a registered trademark of
Hymns Ancient & Modern Ltd
13A Hellesdon Park Road, Norwich,
Norfolk NR6 5DR, UK

British Library Cataloguing in Publication data

A catalogue record for this book is available
from the British Library

ISBN 978-1-78622-463-7

Typeset by Regent Typesetting
Printed and bound in Great Britain by
CPI Group (UK) Ltd

Contents

Acknowledgements

I am indebted beyond words to the many hospice patients, church members, relatives, friends and strangers who trusted me with their own thoughts and feelings about death and dying. From them I have learned so much. Not least I acknowledge with loving remembrance the contribution of my late cousin Viv Meehan, whose story is told in the introduction to this book.

My love and thanks to my daughter Dr Jessica Walker, my ever-faithful supporter and judicious unofficial editor.

I would like to thank several generous-hearted people at Canterbury Press: it was affirming to find a group of people who shared my sense of the importance of this topic. Moreover, these good people were willing to help mould my raw ideas into a readable format. For Christine Smith's wisdom in encouraging me to cultivate a degree of theological balance, and for the eyes-for-detail and patience of Rachel Geddes and Linda Carroll, I am very grateful.

Heartfelt thanks are due to my dear friend the late Professor Bernard Moss who encouraged me to keep refining my ideas and my writing and to just keep going, even when publishers were thin on the ground. Everyone should have a Bernard in their lives.

To God be the glory.

For Jessica, my darling girl.

Introduction

Learning How to Die

This book has been written to help people think and talk about their own inevitable death, and it is hoped that anyone reading it will learn how such a task may be approached confidently within the framework of Christian faith. The straightforward style of writing aims to make the ideas contained within its pages accessible to everyone who wants to do some reading about Christian perspectives on death and dying. It was not written with ordained clergy exclusively in mind, nor are they addressed directly in the main text, but it is hoped that those who have responsibility for the pastoral care of others, such as clergy, chaplains and lay pastoral carers, will find the book useful for their ministry. It is especially hoped that it will help them develop the confidence to encourage those in their care to talk about their future death and what that means to them.

However, to be well equipped to support others in talking about death, it is always helpful for practitioners to consider first these things for themselves, and it is not known whether professional pastoral carers routinely do much thinking about their own death. In one way it is slightly curious that those who take funerals and give support to many grieving people may not have explored the prospect of their own death very much. Yet in another way this is not so surprising because, after all, we are all part of a society where such thinking and such conversations are not commonplace.

One way of getting into this whole topic might be to ask: How much do we actually know about death? Of course, everyone knows that one day they will die, just as they know that on one particular day they were born, but many may not know much about what might be termed the 'mechanics' of how death will happen. One reason for this is that nowadays death tends to happen within a medical setting where such matters can be safely left in the hands of the professionals. Death and dying have become medicalized and we've become used to this fact.

Notwithstanding the normalization of death within a medical facility, it is reasonable to wonder whether the many people who end their days in such a place have arrived there not by design but almost by accident, and to wonder whether anyone ever asked them if that was where they wanted to go to end their days. Did they ever tell anyone what they wanted to happen at the end? Have we discussed our own wants and desires for our death? In the majority of cases the answer to all these questions will be a resounding 'no'. However, if – now we think about it – we would very much like the opportunity to talk with our loved ones about all kinds of things relating to our death – such as how we feel about dying, how we feel about our nearest and dearest, and what we want to happen to us at the end of our lives – then we need to find ways to make a conversation happen. We may need to learn how to do this and we may also need to learn how to do so before it's too late – that is, while we are still in a fit state to do so – rather than postponing it until we are too physically and emotionally strained to think straight, let alone express ourselves in a lucid manner. This book will help the reader to think about these things.

It must be emphasized, though, that the book is not primarily concerned with medical matters at the end of life, such as the kind of final medical interventions that may or may not be wanted. Of course, these kinds of medical considerations may be fiercely important to some people when considering their own death, and this might form part of a conversation about the end of life. Indeed, it is good that in recent years initiatives such as Advance Decisions to Refuse Treatment and Lasting Power of Attorney for Personal Welfare have been developed to address such concerns. So the book is not about medical matters per se; nor does it focus on planning a funeral or how to write a will. Those things are important, but they are not the focus here.

The book is about something more basic: facing the simple fact that human beings are mortal, and taking time to reflect on that reality. It is concerned with becoming more thoughtful about mortality, and perhaps more comfortable with it. Armed with an acceptance of mortality and what that means for Christians, the book then goes on to discuss how helpful conversations about death can be encouraged. Such conversations can vary greatly in content. Some may focus on practical matters such as the kind of end-of-life care an individual may want, or financial and other practical issues, but they may also include spiritual and emotional matters around relationships with others and with God.

My motivation in writing this book

My personal desire to encourage people to think and talk about their future death grew from two different influences on my life: one related to the fact that I am a member of the clergy and the other because I am a member of a family. The clergy-related influence arises from the several years of my life I spent working as a hospice chaplain. During that time, I spent many hours listening to patients who were coming to the end of their lives and learning from them the important things they wanted to say and do in the time they had left. So many patients wanted to talk to someone about their imminent death. Some found ready listeners, others found awkward silence, and – sadly – some found they were 'closed down' by others as soon as they tried to broach the subject. My chaplaincy work eventually led to a PhD research study in which I explored the views of hospice patients, carers and staff around talking about choosing a place to die. One of the findings of this study was that people who are dying often wanted to talk about their oncoming death, even though this might mean exposing themselves and their loved ones to deep emotions. Yet risking the upset that talking might cause to others was deemed worth it in order for their voices to be heard. Some found comfort through this; others found their sense of agency (and even their worth) was affirmed.

So over the years I became convinced that talking about the end of life is a good and helpful thing to do. Furthermore, I began to see that this should not be restricted to hospice patients. We are all mortal; we all face the same end, so why not start this work of facing the fact of our death before we are terminally ill? The more I thought about it, the more I came to see that it could be beneficial to do this work long before we arrive at the last stage of our life. Indeed, none of us can predict with any certainty what the last stage of life will be like or when it will be. For example, no one can predict whether they will undergo a prolonged period of decline or whether they will die suddenly or in the prime of life. If someone decides to wait until they are near the very end, they may miss their chance to talk. Of course, talking about the end of life might not be easy but I remain convinced that it is a helpful thing to do.

As a Christian, I wondered what role faith would play in approaching this task. I wondered whether faith in Jesus would make people especially equipped and ready to think and talk about their death and, if so, why this might be. Christian faith encompasses every aspect of life, including death and even life beyond death, but I wondered whether these beliefs would actually provide Christians with the practical skills to enable them to contemplate their death. So the Christian perspective on death and dying became very much part of my ruminations, and I hope that the book will add something to Christian views on this topic. In particular, I hope that it will say something pertinent and interesting to fellow clergy, lay chaplains and pastoral carers.

The second influence on my growing interest in promoting conversations about death arose from conversations with a family member who was approaching death. These conversations proved formative in the development of my ideas, and it is hoped that the recounting of such a personal story will provide some background to the thoughts presented here. To this end, the following few paragraphs briefly relate my experience and my reflections on it.

When my cousin Viv told me she had just a few weeks left to live, the whole topic of death suddenly became very personal. No longer was I the chaplain offering compassionate care to patients. I was now the grieving relative having to negotiate all the raw emotions, and this experience inevitably drowned any residual professional detachment. Heartachingly painful as it was, the conversations I had with my lovely, dying cousin taught me that things needed to be said and they needed to be said now before it was too late. I was not ready for Viv to die and leave me. But she *was* dying and there was nothing I could do about that. It had to be faced and I will for ever be thankful that she had the good sense and determination to make me listen to what she needed to say.

Importantly, there were things that Viv desperately wanted to happen during her last days, and there were some things that she absolutely did *not* want to happen. The problem was that other family members refused to hear what she urgently wanted to say. Looking back, it seems that the thought of losing her was too much for them. Their grief and anguish made them too distressed and distracted to even consider talking to her about her imminent death in a straightforward way. It was bad enough that they were losing her; the last thing they wanted to do was talk about it. Seemingly, they felt the best thing to do would be just to get on with the practical stuff: to stay busy and at all costs stay positive. So they nailed a smile to their faces whenever they were dealing with her, and whatever was happening everyone tried not to cry in the firm belief that it was not going to help anyone.

So instead of talking to Viv about her oncoming death and embracing all that it meant, including the profound sadness of separation, there was an atmosphere of forced cheeriness because this was deemed 'kind'. This would help her 'keep her chin up'. However, Viv was desperate to tell us, her family, certain things, and because we weren't listening she felt powerless. For example, all sorts of people wanted to visit Viv in her last days. But she did not want the house full of relatives and friends she hadn't seen for years, now that she was experiencing symptoms that kept her in the bathroom for much of the day. In fact, she was never one to be embarrassed about bodily functions but she was keenly aware that this might not be very nice for visitors. She was such a caring person throughout her life and although now she was the one requiring care, it was so typical of her that, even at this point, she was considering everyone else's needs.

Moreover, she was still able to express her care, if only we'd give her half a chance. This was so typical of Viv and it reminded me of all the times in my life that she'd always found a way to express love and affection, even when other family members could not or would not do this. Like many families, we experienced various times of falling out of love with one another, and some of these periods were stark and painful. When certain family members refused to talk to each other and you had to be careful what you said, she would still phone me up to remind me that she loved me. I don't want to claim that Viv was some sort of saint because, like the rest of us, she was far from perfect, but she really wanted to do some good things for us at the end.

One of the things she wanted to do was to give some of her clothes and possessions away to particular people in the family. She felt that this would give her great comfort and even a sense of joy. But no one would let her talk about this stuff. I'm absolutely certain that no one was trying to be unkind, but their behaviour blocked her wishes from being carried out and left her with feelings of frustration, failure and powerlessness. What would happen is this: when Viv would try to offer someone a particular dress or piece of jewellery, the recipient would just get incredibly upset. Viv would then back off and end up comforting the other person by saying things like, 'OK, then, it doesn't matter, we'll talk another day.' At first glance it could appear that the things she was so desperate to share were rather trivial: she didn't have riches to give away, just the usual flotsam and jetsam accumulated over an ordinary lifetime, but this was not about possessions. Viv was reaching out to us at a time when she was, very likely, feeling isolated. What she needed at that time was for us to work with her, not against her.

Eventually I worked out that this was not about me and my grief, but supremely about Viv and, most importantly of all, I realized that this was a now-or-never situation: that I had this one and only opportunity, a once-in-a-lifetime one, to do these last things for her. Only then was I able to quell the raging voice in my head that wanted to shout 'Please don't talk about the end' and tried instead to concentrate on just listening to what she was saying. I understood that this was not the time to try to argue her out of her opinions, but to simply learn about and accept what she wanted to do and to try to make that happen. I didn't always find this easy because it meant letting go of doing things my way. For example, it meant not visiting at certain times and not doing some things I wanted to do for her, such as sing a song or do her hair. But once I put my own agenda to one side, I found that I got to appreciate her more in those last days. I got to serve her in the ways she actually needed, not in the ways that I thought she needed. I was able to look after her actual needs rather than the needs I perceived she had.

In the end she was ready to die. None of us were really ready to let her go: but she'd come to the end of it. I learnt that by listening to her. Because Viv had been able to talk about her imminent death and I was able to listen to her, I came to see that she had insight into what she wanted to communicate as death approached and how she wanted to spend her last days. I know she had not discussed this with anyone at an earlier stage in her life, but it seemed that as she entered the terminal phase she simply learnt how to go about it – that is, she learnt how to die and had attempted to ask her family to simply accompany her as she did what she had to do.

The phrase 'learning how to die' was reputedly coined by Leonardo da Vinci who, apparently, said that while he thought he'd been learning how to live he had in fact been learning how to die. I found myself wondering what might give a Christian the confidence to learn how to die. I wondered what knowledge and skills might need to be acquired in order to face death with at least some degree of assurance. Christian beliefs about death and what comes after would surely be supremely important in this regard. This is explored at some length in Chapter 2, but by way of introduction the section below offers some broad brushstrokes of theological views on death, dying and resurrection as a means of locating the subject matter of this book – that is, talking about death within a Christian framework.

Death, dying and resurrection in Christian thought

It is a fundamental part of humanity that we are mortal: in some ways death and dying define humanity. Dying or being dead may be described as the time when bodily functions cease irreversibly. The Bible just accepts this as fact; for example, Ecclesiastes 3.2 says that there is a time to die and Hebrews 9.27 states that it is appointed for mortals to die. At the same time, the Bible is not neutral about death: the foremost reason given for mortality is contained in the story of the expulsion of Adam and Eve from the garden of Eden (Gen. 3).

This account in Genesis offers a means of making sense of the presence of evil and death in human life. Written at a time when the people of God were experiencing the pain of exile, it perhaps is no surprise that the story of Adam and Eve sees death as essentially alienation and separation, often self-inflicted. Through this story, the Bible posits that death became part of the human condition as a result of Adam and Eve's disobedience to God in their turning away from the order of things as outlined by God (Gen. 3.2–3). One result of Adam and Eve's being banished from the garden was a new state of enmity between humanity and the natural world (Gen. 3.15–19). Additionally, and most significantly, their transgressive behaviour subsequently destined Adam and Eve to one day return to the dust from which they came; in other words, from now on their eventual fate would be death (Gen. 3.19). With Adam and Eve standing as archetypes, their sad fate became the fate of the whole of humanity. Henceforth, human beings would know death.

Nevertheless, throughout the Old Testament we see God working to undo the separation of Eden, binding himself to humanity in the Covenant, continually calling us back to relationship through the prophets and acting in human history to save his people. Ultimately, God comes in Christ to overcome finally all that separates us from him. There are no lengths to which God in Christ will not go to redeem us, including facing death. This is a statement of great importance. Because Christian faith is always Christ-centred, this simple yet profound fact is key: that in Jesus, the immortal God chose to experience human death. This is an immense truth to ponder, for in experiencing death Jesus stands in solidarity with all humanity. As the writer of the letter to the Hebrews puts it, Jesus was fully human in every way (Heb. 2.17) and by God's grace he tasted death for everyone (Heb. 2.9). Likewise, the reason that the lamb of the book of Revelation chapter 5 is deemed worthy to receive honour, glory and praise is because he is the lamb that was slain (Rev. 5.11).

Jesus' experience of a mortal death, then, gives confidence that can make a difference to the fact that one day everyone must enter the experience of death. Death and dying, inescapable realities for every human being, essential parts of human materiality, are somehow united with the materiality of Jesus, who is not only the anointed one, the Christ, but also Emmanuel, God with us, God incarnate. As the prologue to John's Gospel so eloquently puts it, the Word became flesh and lived among us (John 1.14). The doctrine of the incarnation speaks powerfully about how, in Jesus, almighty God chooses to inhabit weak, frail, finite, vulnerable flesh. Our materiality matters to God. Human birth, growing, living and dying matter to God. Death matters to God.

Arguably, the most poignant depiction of God's deep pastoral concern for human death is when Jesus weeps at the grave of his friend Lazarus (John 11.35). In this passage (John 11.1–44), we see Jesus display great emotion in response to Martha and Mary's sadness and distress at the loss of their dear brother. This exquisite expression of grief underlines Jesus' full humanity and points to his role as the man of sorrows who is 'acquainted with grief' (Isa. 53.3 RSV). With those who stand at graves and weep, in Jesus, God stands alongside in solidarity and sympathy.

Furthermore, given that Jesus' crucifixion was just days away, it would not be surprising if Jesus the man was, at this moment, also moved by pre-emptive grief for his own impending death. Because Lazarus' restoration to life is seen as provoking the religious leaders into finally taking action to kill Jesus, his tears at Lazarus' grave could be seen as similar to his anticipatory sorrow and anguish in the synoptic Gospels' garden of Gethsemane scenes (Mark 14.32–42; Matt. 26.36–46; Luke 22.40–46). At Lazarus' grave, then, we see revealed in Jesus God's empathetic understanding of the enormity of human death.

At the same time, Jesus' tears may also indicate a further source of distress. Jesus weeps because death is present in creation: it mars its beauty and the creator's original purpose. Jeffrey John (2001, p. 219) asserts that the Greek word used for Jesus' deep distress can also indicate tears of anger as well as grief, and so Jesus is deeply moved and even angry at the powers of evil that cause sickness, death and grief. This is not how things are meant to be. The colossal price of the grace required to set things right is somewhat foreshadowed in these tears, as the cost of redemption entails the death of the saviour.

Indeed, the centrality of Jesus' death in Christian theology cannot be overstated. The foremost symbol of the faith worn as jewellery, depicted in art and utilized in devotion is the cross, the gallows on which Jesus was put to death. The narrative of the death and resurrection of Jesus, the passion narrative, sits at the heart of each Gospel, and many writers think this was the first and most important part of the Jesus story that was initially taught to seekers and new believers. Certainly, in the early preaching of the Church, as recounted in the Acts of the Apostles, it is this event that looms large (see, for example, Acts 2.14–36ff.; 4.8–12; 5.29–32). Most holy communion liturgies across all Christian traditions are seen as memorials or remembrances of Jesus' death on the cross. In them, it is not only Jesus' last supper that is represented: the death of Jesus is clearly seen as integral to the sacrament. Through the liturgy we are reminded that it was Jesus' last supper because it took place the night before he died. It is not merely a memorable Passover meal; instead, the superlative sacrament of the world-wide Church is intimately bound up with the fact that Jesus died.

Apart from this being a required part of his humanity, the reasons why Jesus died and what Jesus' death achieved is a huge and important theological topic that is generally referred to as the doctrine of atonement. Put very simply and briefly, atonement (or at-one-ment) concerns a process by which reconciliation with God is achieved by the removal of sin that has resulted in separation between human beings and God. This separation caused by sin is well depicted in the expulsion of Adam and Eve from the garden of Eden into a world where, as we have already noted, death will be a reality (Gen. 3.23). In contrast to the time of creation that God had declared as good, after their expulsion Adam and Eve soon learnt that separation from God is not good. In order to overcome such separation, atonement was required.

In the Old Testament and indeed in the time of Jesus, the Jewish system of sacrifice was understood to achieve the required atonement, at least in a temporary way. However, the rituals needed to be repeated every year by the high priest on behalf of the people. The Christian view of atonement states that Jesus' death on the cross achieved atonement once and for all so that problems and estrangement between humanity and

God would then be resolved. Importantly, it is God-in-Christ who achieves the atonement, not people themselves. And what God does in Christ, of course, is die. Taking up the Jewish sacrifice imagery, John describes Jesus as the lamb of God who takes away the sins of the world (John 1.29). Referring to the problem of sin and the need for atonement, St Paul says that all humanity is caught up in sin, in Adam all die (1 Cor. 15.22), but because Christ died for our sins the effects of Adam's sins have been nullified (1 Cor. 15.3; Rom. 5.12–21).

Down through the years – and still today – varying views about exactly how Jesus' death achieved atonement have been held. Some have favoured the imagery of redemption, with a price being paid to release humanity, which was captive to sin (e.g. Eph. 1.7; Col. 1.14; Heb. 9.12; Rom. 3.24). Proponents of this view have included the early Church 'fathers' Origen and Augustine. Others have found the image of substitution helpful, whereby the penalty due for sinful behaviour is dealt with by Jesus' death (e.g. Rom. 3.23–26; 2 Cor. 5.21; 1 Pet. 2.24; 3.18). This view very much came to the fore with the sixteenth-century reformers Luther and Calvin. The image of Jesus becoming victorious over sin by his death is also very apparent in the New Testament (e.g. 1 Cor. 15.54–56; Col. 2.15; 2 Tim. 1.10; Rom. 6.9). This is sometimes referred to as 'Christus Victor' and was popularized for a time in the twentieth century by Gustaf Aulen, who embraced this notion as the title of his book (Aulen, 1931). This motif persists in hymnody, from Wesley's risen conquering Son of 'Thine Be the Glory' to Getty and Townend's conquering risen Christ in their hymn 'See What A Morning'. Whichever stance on atonement is adopted by theologians, all agree that it is Jesus' death that achieves it. Many would be able to align themselves with C. S. Lewis's conclusion that no explanation of the atonement is as relevant as the fact of the atonement (Lewis, 1952, p. 54).

Christian theology never underestimates that death deals in loss and is therefore the cause of much human grief, which can be extremely upsetting. Death is seen as the last enemy (1 Cor. 15.26), as containing a sting (1 Cor. 15.55–56), and a time is looked for when God will wipe away all tears of grief from people's eyes (Rev. 21.4; Isa. 25.8). The biblical and theological recognition of the reality of grief caused by death is helpful in ensuring a pastorally sensitive response towards those who are grieving. It also helps to point to the fact that, of course, it is not just the death of Jesus that is important because the Jesus story does not end with his death. Wonderfully, the story moves on to his resurrection, his being raised from the dead to a new sort of life.

The resurrection of Jesus is the basis for Christian belief in the possibility that human beings can also experience this new life beyond the grave. This is an extremely important theological point. As St Paul puts it, if Christ has not been raised, our preaching is useless and so is your faith (1 Cor. 15.14). With Jesus as the prototype, the resurrection re-orders how death and life with God must consequently be understood. Death does not have the final word: through the resurrection there is a new life to come. The resurrection gives rise to a new way of assessing the significance of death – and indeed life. Although it does not prevent human beings from dying, the resurrection of Jesus means that death can now be seen differently (Evans and Davison, 2014). For example, death need no longer be feared because through the resurrection Jesus has destroyed the power of death and freed all those who were held in slavery by the fear of it (Heb. 2.14–15). Believers need fear death no more, as where Jesus has led – that is, through death and into the resurrection life – they will surely follow (Col. 1.22–23; 1 Cor. 6.14).

Furthermore, the newness and quality of the resurrection life has its own powerful appeal. For example, the resurrection body will be imperishable, glorious and powerful, no longer subject to mortal weakness as a result of illness and inevitable ageing and decay (1 Cor. 15.42). Jesus himself said that when people rise from the dead they are like angels in heaven (Mark 12.25; Luke 20.36). Such thought touches on theological ideas about the material world. Earlier we noted that implicit in the incarnation is the notion that human materiality – which of course includes death – is a matter that concerns God deeply. The resurrection of the body of Jesus, and the promise of such a resurrection for believers, is consistent with such theology: it is part of God's ongoing concern for the people he has created, who have a tangible physicality.

The resurrection also addresses humanity's broken relationship with the natural world as a result of the fall. Hence in Christian theology, resurrection life is associated with the renewal of the entire cosmos. In Pauline thought the creation will be set free from its bondage to decay (Rom. 8.21), because in the resurrection God's power to transform all materiality has been revealed (Phil. 3.21). The new heaven and new earth envisaged by Peter, and John the writer of Revelation, convey a similar idea (2 Pet. 3.13; Rev. 21.1 and 5).

This very positive theology gives rise to great hope for Christians. Although death is difficult it does not signify the ultimate end, even though at first glance it may appear to do so. However, faith looks beyond death and looks forward to resurrection life. This has been the unswerving teaching of the Church down the ages. Credal formulas and statements of faith across all traditions include something expectant and encouraging about the resurrection. The Nicene Creed, which is accepted as authoritative by the Roman Catholic, Eastern Orthodox, Anglican and major Protestant churches, proclaims that Christians look for the resurrection of the dead and the life of the world to come (Church of England, 2002), while the Apostles' Creed, widely accepted in Western Christianity, speaks about the resurrection of the body (Church of England, 2002).

Such hopeful theology underpins this book. I firmly believe that thinking about death and talking about it in the light of such hope offers a constructive means of apprehending afresh all that God has to offer in terms of his total care for his creatures and his creation. Furthermore, I believe that gaining confidence to talk about such matters gives Christians something positive to offer the world. Talking about death may not come easily, but I believe that learning how to go about it is utterly worthwhile.

I

Talking About Death and Dying Can Be Difficult

Leonardo da Vinci is reputed to have said, 'While I thought I was learning how to live I have been learning how to die'. For me, these words resonate with so much truth about what it means to be human and what it means to be a Christian. Both aspects, living and dying, are part of the human equation. Therefore, it seems to follow that both living and dying require our attention but it is unclear how much weight we should give to each factor of the equation. Rightly, so much human effort is expended in learning how to live. We grow up, we learn about the world of work, we form all kinds of relationships, we make homes and pursue hobbies and interests, we may become parents and grandparents. This is the stuff of life and what we do in life seems to be what is valued.

Nowhere is this clearer than in many contemporary funeral eulogies, which seem to comprise, almost to the exclusion of all else, the reciting of the elements of a life well lived and not squandered. In such an address we hear about achievements and awards gained, how the person progressed through the ranks of their chosen profession and how they became part of a burgeoning family. Tales of their many contributions to their local community through acts of charity or sporting prowess are offered as proofs of the substance of their existence. They are held up to us all as an example of someone who knew how to live. While such a recitation may be comforting to the mourners and potentially inspiring to all, it surely addresses only one aspect of what it means to have lived and then died.

I recognize the above scenario well. When I was a young minister, my mentor decided he'd like to come along and observe how I conducted funerals. So he attended one where I delivered what I considered to be a well-balanced and sensitive eulogy of the deceased. The family were grateful and appreciative of the care I'd taken to portray the life of one whom they loved. So I looked forward to receiving similar approving comments from my mentor. He did, in fact, compliment my presentation skills and considerate treatment of the dead person's life story, but he held the firm view that I had given a rather lopsided address considering this was a Christian funeral. His judgement was that I'd missed an opportunity to gently and respectfully preach the gospel and to give a clear account of the Christian hope on which our funeral liturgy – and indeed our faith – is founded. In so doing I'd missed the opportunity to put this person's death into the eternal context. I'd failed to give enough weight to the meaning of death within the Christian world view. To paraphrase Leonardo, I'd concentrated too much on the significance of living to the detriment of the consequence of dying.

In trying to understand why I did this I came to the uncomfortable conclusion that I found it much easier to talk about life than death and dying. I wondered whether it was death in general that made me avoid the subject or whether it was the thought that one day, hopefully at some time in the very distant future, it would surely be me lying in a box in a church with some minister talking about my life. I felt strangely heartened by Karl Barth's famous observation that, 'One day a company of people will make their way to a churchyard and lay a coffin in the ground, then all go home again. Except that one of them will not come back and that will be me' (Barth, 1966, p. 117). For me, this served as a reminder that although death may be a difficult and potentially upsetting subject, it is a reality that I, along with the rest of humanity, must one day face.

For we will all die: that much is certain. It seems so prosaic to say that, but somehow it needs to be written down and said out loud to one another in order to help us face the simple, hard fact that at the end of our lives we will die. We can choose to be inspired by Leonardo and seize the opportunity to prepare for this momentous event, to learn how to die, or we can decline the opportunity and ignore the prospect until it is finally forced on us. We can, if we so choose, live much of our lives in a state of denial, avoiding all thought of death. If we think about death at all it will somehow concern other people but will not apply to us. We can tell ourselves that our concern is the business of living and we can put our trust – and perhaps even our hope – in medical science, which can surely be relied on to repair and sustain life almost perpetually. Well, almost. But the truth remains that no one can avoid death for ever.

Although it may be painful to think about it, death is a defining part of the human condition and it is an event towards which we are all moving. If we find this hard to face, it may help to explore why this should be so and then, armed with understanding, begin to formulate strategies to help us think about death and dying in more positive ways and within a meaningful framework.

As a starting point for this I have found it immensely helpful to recognize that thinking about my future death can evoke strong feelings of grief and loss in me *now*. When I think about the fact that I will die, it's as if I start to grieve for myself, in advance. And I'm more than a little reluctant to take on this task. No one actively wants to do the work of grieving because no one wants to lose that which they are grieving for. It's just something that has to be done. It's not a pleasant experience, and although we may grow through it in all kinds of ways, it's not something we look forward to because it's upsetting, difficult and disruptive. However, we are familiar with its pathways and we know that people come through it and out the other side. We are all accustomed to grieving for others and we have more than likely acquired some skills in this area.

What is more, we are skilled at dealing with a whole range of losses that will occur in a lifetime, with their accompanying feelings of intense sadness and grief. The kinds of losses we may have to negotiate could include the world of work, relationships or health, for example. Perhaps we've been made redundant and incurred the loss of wealth and status. Or perhaps a relationship has come to an end and for a while we've been utterly bereft of comfort. Illness may have meant we have lost a certain physical or mental capacity and our sense of self-worth has taken a battering. Through such experiences we come to know the painful emotions and negative thoughts that characterize sharp encounters with grief and loss. We are, to coin a phrase, 'acquainted with grief' (Isa. 53.3 RSV).

Therefore, I suggest that we accept that when we start to think about our own future death, we will grieve: we will be sorrowful. Having accepted that, we can then start to think about how we can get through this grief or at least cope with it enough to be able to deal with other important aspects associated with our eventual death. For instance, we may need to leave our self-grief to one side in order to concentrate on making provision for those we will leave behind.

For the moment, then, let us consider what might equip us to contend with the ultra-personal self-grief that may engulf us for a while.

Thinking about your death as a kind of loss

Helpfully, much has been written about the difficulties of facing and coping with loss, especially within the context of bereavement and terminal illness, and insights from various theories of loss have much to offer us. Theories of loss can help us understand thoughts and feelings that may arise as we begin to face the inevitability of our own death. Therefore, let us briefly consider the work of three significant thinkers in this area.

Elisabeth Kübler-Ross's seminal and hugely influential work on death and dying argues that it takes time for people to accept the thought of dying (1969, p. 236). She outlines five stages of grief through which people move when faced with the prospect of death. These are: denial; anger; bargaining;

depression; and, finally, acceptance. During the Denial Stage people will say to themselves, 'This is not happening to me', and they will continue to live their lives as they did before. When they reach the Anger Stage they may ask questions such as, 'Why me?', and may feel a sense of rage that this has happened. The Bargaining Stage is characterized by feelings of, 'Yes, it's happening to me but maybe if I'm good it won't really happen.' Often people plead with God or some sort of higher power. During the Depression Stage feelings of hopelessness, frustration and bitterness – sometimes leading to thoughts of suicide – can be very real. Finally, there comes Acceptance, which is not mere resignation to death but an ability to look forward and enjoy life while it remains.

Over the years, this Stages of Grief Model has been refined and critiqued as some have questioned whether there is an automatic linear progression through the various stages or whether people's lived experience is a much more back-and-forth affair. Bernard Moss argues that the concept of acceptance is much more complex than this simple word might suggest (2005, p. 47).

William Worden rejects the notion of grief as a passive progression of stages through which a person is carried (2009, p. 26). Rather, he sees mourners as active agents within the grief experience and encourages them to exercise their power by actively engaging with the loss that they are facing. He describes four tasks of grief: accepting the loss; acknowledging the pain of the loss; adjusting to a new environment; and reinvesting in the reality of a new life. In Worden's scheme, the tasks of grief are not states of achievement but a fluctuating process through which a new normal life will be accommodated without that which was lost.

Margaret Stroebe and Henk Schut (1999) developed the Dual Process Model of Grief whereby the mourner experiences two different ways of behaving: a loss-orientated way and a restoration-orientated way. Stroebe and Schut believe that as we grieve we oscillate between these two different modes of being. The loss-orientated mode is characterized by feelings of sadness, loneliness, anxiety, depression and even despair, while the restoration-orientated mode comprises acceptance of the loss, the relinquishing of associated attachments and a focusing on the reality of the new life to come. The Dual Process Model recognizes that people may function fairly normally in their lives while at the same time experience periods of grief. Eventually there will be a greater future focus, but there is a recognition that events may still trigger a return to the loss-orientated mode at any moment.

A common theme in these theories of loss is that there is a process through which people move. According to such theories, it takes time to accommodate thoughts and feelings generated by loss, and we may find some aspects of these theories of loss helpful in assessing our particular attitude to the prospect of our eventual death.

It must also be acknowledged that for some people death seems to be such a confounding idea that they just cannot make it fit in with their world view. Steven Heine and colleagues (2006) believe that many people will never fully resolve in themselves the fact that they will die. For such people, making decisions about how they want to face death are, if not impossible, immensely difficult to actualize.

I was faced with a very clear example of this kind of thinking when I was a hospice chaplain. I had been asked to visit a gentleman who had been given a terminal diagnosis and a very short prognosis, meaning the doctors thought he had just a few weeks left. As this gentleman lived alone on a remote farm in the local moorlands, it was thought that he should be offered a place in the hospice to spend his final days so he could be looked after. A nurse had previously been dispatched to explain this offer, but had come back without having been able to discuss the difficult fact that this man's life would soon come to an end. So the chaplain was sent out next.

I was met with the usual country hospitality of a very large and very strong mug of tea in the kitchen and we talked about this and that. After sympathizing about the recent closure of the local cattle market, meaning that farmers now had to travel all the way to Leek to buy and sell livestock, I brought the conversation round to the state of this gentleman's health. I explained very clearly that the hospice could provide a place in which he could die if that was his wish. I'll never forget the incredulous look he gave me as he said with utter equanimity, 'Lass, why on earth are you telling me that?' I replied that it was because of his medical condition and the fact that it was thought that this would soon begin to deteriorate. Again he met me with indifference and simply said, 'But I hope not to get any worse.' And that was the end of our conversation.

Obviously, he never came into the hospice. Perhaps he had faced his oncoming death in his own way and for him the sort of planning that I'd suggested was simply irrelevant. He certainly did not admit to any kind of self-grief or sadness in advance of his death. After his death, however, there was still work to be done. Because he'd left no instructions regarding a funeral, this had to be handled by the local authority, as did the selling of the farm and the settling of the estate. This may give us pause regarding the state of affairs we wish to leave behind. While it may be argued that this man was successful in blocking conversations he clearly did not wish to have, there were certain consequences to his actions. If we wish our own death to follow a different path from the one he took, we may consider it worthwhile to decide to talk about the fact that we will inevitably deteriorate and one day we will die.

Some contemporary views on talking about the end of life

A number of contemporary thinkers see value in adopting a more accepting attitude towards death. Like the stoics of old, some point to the life-enhancing effects of embracing mortality here and now. They argue that fully accepting the fact you're going to die can help you make the most of your life. William Irvine describes this process as 'confronting the darkness that is death' (2009, p. 42). He recommends not pulling the curtains over the darkness that lurks beyond the window, but rather staring straight into it so that when you turn away you're thankful for the light. This accords with the views of some terminally ill people who report that facing their own mortality enabled them to focus their minds on making the most of every day they had left.

But you don't have to be terminally ill to think in this way. I knew someone in the prime of life who had put off writing their will for many years because they just could not face thinking about their own death. Making provision for their family after they'd gone was always there in the back of their mind, troubling them, but they felt that writing a will would be a morbid and depressing thing to do. However, when their favourite charity started offering a free will-writing service they were persuaded to take the plunge. After successfully and painlessly writing their will they said they felt released to get on with the rest of their life. They didn't need to keep thinking about death; now they could truly concentrate on living.

Caitlin Doughty, the author of *Smoke Gets In Your Eyes* (2014), started her career as a crematorium assistant and now campaigns to change what she regards as the developed world's death-avoiding culture. She argues that thinking about your death can move you closer to magnanimity. She admits that it may take time to develop such a view, as thinking about death can stir up very strong and sometimes negative emotions within us. However, her view is that over time you can come to terms with the notion that ultimately you will have to give your body, your atoms and molecules, back to the universe when you've finished with them. Moreover, she regards this process as having a positive effect on one's outlook.

Others argue for a more accepting attitude towards death in order for plans to be made in advance and for support to be accessed both before the death as well as afterwards. Andrew Marshall (2017a), who wrote a memoir about his experience of grief after his partner died, was motivated in part by his view that we are not generally taught how to accept death and how to move on from a loss, despite the fact that death is a universal experience (Marshall, 2017b). He believes that such a death-denying culture means that bereaved people and those caring for loved ones at the end of their lives often lack the support they need because people tiptoe around the subject and talk in euphemisms. Marshall therefore advocates a more open addressing of the subject to make it easier for people to seek help. Moreover, he believes that a society that takes on board a franker approach to death could become more skilled at providing appropriate support when it is most needed.

A growing number of doctors and other healthcare professionals are working to advance conversations around end-of-life care. The bestselling American author and surgeon Atul Gawande, for example, champions more discussions about death between doctors and patients. Drawing on events leading up to his father's death, Gawande recounts his utter disappointment at healthcare professionals' reluctance to have open discussions with his father about this (2015, p. 243). His experience was that those caring for his father did not exactly deny that death was near; they simply avoided bringing the subject up. Should the subject rear its ugly head, it was neatly sidestepped by focusing the discussion on medical matters such as treatment options. He believes that doctors and other clinicians need to seriously improve their practice in helping people face the fact that their life is finite. The argument goes that if we all want to be the authors of our own stories, we should give due attention to how the story ends.

However, it must also be recognized that not all medical practitioners avoid the topic of death when talking with their patients. Palliative care is a medical specialty that explicitly focuses on end-of-life matters. This discipline has long upheld and promoted the belief that dying is a normal and natural process. Indeed, an open acknowledgement that palliative-care patients have a terminal diagnosis is key to such care. The UK National Institute for Clinical Excellence (NICE) has recently described palliative care as the holistic and total care of someone who is approaching the end of life, combined with offering care to the patient's family and carers (NICE, 2004). In the palliative world, patients are increasingly encouraged to get involved in planning for their deaths, and this approach is slowly spreading to other healthcare settings such as hospital wards and care homes.

Summary

The various views in this chapter give us much to consider: it seems that a debate is underway in society regarding talking openly about the end of our lives. We may not yet know where we, personally, stand with this. Importantly, Christian faith has much to contribute to the debate. So let us now consider Christian approaches to thinking about the end of our lives.

2

Christian Approaches to Talking About Death and Dying

At first glance, it may seem that because Christian faith includes belief in life beyond death, talking about death and dying will be straightforward. It may seem that because faith carries us to life beyond death, Christians don't need to avoid death-talk and can confidently face death head-on. The central and unique tenets of Christianity teach that Jesus looked death squarely in the face, experienced it, went through it and came out the other side with a message of hope, and delivered the power by which believers can apprehend this hope and courage. Christian faith is, supremely, resurrection faith. We follow a God who thoroughly embraced the reality of death, by dying for us himself in the person of Jesus Christ. Moreover, he then rose from the dead to offer us hope of a new kind of life with God that is beyond death and for all eternity. For Christians, the reality of death and dying expressed in the cross of Christ is foundational. So too is the hope of the resurrection. As Karl Barth says, Christians have 'a beyond' to look forward to: for Christians, death is not the end (1966, pp. 117–18). Logically, then, death need not be feared.

However, Christians, like all other people, are not merely logical beings and so casting fear aside may be easier said than done. It may be helpful to explore what the 'beyond' looks like. While the Bible does not give all the details about what life after death entails, it offers some information that gives rise to hope and potentially courage in the face of death. Some of this relates to what happened to the person of Jesus himself.

The resurrection appearances of Jesus recorded in the Gospels reveal that, beyond death, Jesus attained a new physical reality. He had a real body of flesh and blood that, as the women at the tomb and Thomas discovered, could be touched. The women at the tomb fell at his feet and took hold of him (John 20.17), and later in the upper room Jesus invited Thomas to put his hands in the nail marks in his hands and side (John 20.27). The Gospel accounts also reveal that this body could consume food – for example, when Jesus eats supper with the two disciples at Emmaus (Luke 24.30) and when he shares breakfast with them on the beach (John 21.10–14). So there is a bodily resurrection, but this is not mere resuscitation with everything remaining as before: there is a new body. An indication that things are the same yet very different can be found in the fact that Jesus' body can now apparently pass through walls, as he did when he appeared to the disciples who were hiding in a locked room (John 20.19). He was also now able to disappear as he did at Emmaus after he had broken bread at the table (Luke 24.30–31).

Most encouragingly, Jesus' resurrection body, though still bearing the marks of his former suffering, has been healed. His scars are visible yet they no longer have the power to hurt, to maim and to kill. After his resurrection, Jesus has a new physicality: one that has transcended pain, suffering and death. For him these things are no more, as he has been raised to a new kind of life with a new kind of bodily existence.

The early Church clearly looked to what happened to Jesus as a sign and foretaste of what would happen to believers after death. St Paul confidently talks about the resurrection of the dead and how the dead in Christ will be raised imperishable as the mortal body gives way to an immortal one (1 Cor. 15.52–53), and John asserts that when Jesus appears again at some future point, we shall be like him (1 John 3.2). From the outset Christians have believed that Jesus' resurrection body serves as the model for our fate beyond death. The very last book of the Bible, Revelation, completes the New Testament view that our new resurrected physical bodies will equip us for life in that place where there will be no more pain and death (Rev. 21.4). The resurrection of Jesus is the ground of our Christian hope for a life beyond death for ourselves.

However, it is too simplistic and potentially intimidating to suggest that, in light of the biblical view, all Christians can and should glibly accept death and that all Christians are automatically equipped to talk openly about it. In any discussion about death the utmost sensitivity is required if we are not to trample on one another's deeply held feelings and fears. Despite holding firm Christian views, the thought of death can be frightening and painful for some and this must never be underestimated or callously swept aside. Michael Lloyd (2020, pp. 206–8) notes well that the promise of resurrection does not make death something that people can always contemplate with serenity and without a measure of suffering and grief. Perhaps the first important thing that Christian faith has to offer the debate is a compassionate approach that takes account of people's lived experiences of grief. In order to assist people to talk openly about the end of life we must recognize the potential pain involved. This is borne out in real life. No matter how much Christians may profess to look forward to the resurrection, it cannot be denied that they also cry at funerals. And this is more than OK: it is appropriate. I know this to be true in my own life. As we lowered my mother's coffin into the ground and the words about the sure and certain hope of the resurrection were intoned, words that I both believe and cling to, I felt no dissonance as my hot tears cascaded on to the coffin in great drenching drops. On the contrary, I felt that my tears echoed or perhaps amplified the gentle pitter patter of the baptismal water my brother and I had earlier sprinkled over her. Hope of the resurrection and sadness beyond words were, for me, two sides of the same coin, fittingly and easily held together.

So Christians grieve for others. This does not undermine hope in the resurrection, but it must be acknowledged that Christians usually find death sad and sometimes disappointing. All manner of losses have to be negotiated depending on the relationship we had with the person who has died. If a parent dies, most of us have to come to terms with the loss of that bond; if a partner or friend dies, we may have to come to terms with the loss of future plans and dreams. If a leader dies, we may find ourselves bereft of direction for a while. The process of grieving is not foreshortened merely because you profess Christian faith. Grief is part of the human condition and is common to all.

Similarly, when it comes to thinking about our own eventual death, Christians may have to undergo the process of self-grief described in the preceding chapter, as Christian faith does not automatically provide immunity from this. The Bible describes death in negative terms: in the New Testament it is seen as an enemy, the last enemy (1 Cor. 15.26). Notwithstanding that we could not have the resurrection without death, it is still seen as an enemy. Based on 1 Thessalonians 4.13, at every funeral service I have ever taken I have confidently – and, I hope, sympathetically – encouraged people not to grieve as those without hope, but I have never told people not to grieve. Grief is natural and we need to go through it. And I believe this holds true when we contemplate our own future death. Be prepared to grieve if you need to; it's OK to be sad and disappointed, but, in faith, do not grieve as those without hope.

When I have thought about my own death, I have wondered what it is that I'm grieving for. Part of the answer is that I will lose some things that are very dear to me. To use what might seem a flippant illustration, I remember laughing hysterically at a comedy programme which suggested that George W. Bush, then president of the USA, had recently quipped that 'When you die, you lose a major part of your life'! But surely, I thought, when you die you lose *all* of your life. However, I'm now beginning to think that Bush's reputed comment has some truth in it. When I die I will lose some things that I now treasure. I will no longer be able to have the same kind of relationships with those closest to me that I currently enjoy. For example, I will no longer talk on the phone every day with my daughter and I will no longer sleep in the same bed as my husband. These thoughts make me sad. Moreover, the fact that

I don't have a precise idea of what life beyond death will be like is not helpful. I know that now I can only *see through a glass darkly* and that one day I will *see face to face* (1 Cor. 13.12). Sometimes this comforts me and sometimes it does not. What does help is allowing myself to accept that some things that I rely on in this life are hard to let go of and must be offered to God in prayer and trust. Likewise, remembering that Jesus, the resurrection, has prepared a place for me in the Father's house (John 11.25; 14.2) helps me to grieve for myself without letting go of hope.

Christian faith most assuredly offers hope with regard to death and dying. Put simply, Christians believe that death is not the end because Jesus conquered death at Calvary. It is this foundational belief that led St Paul to the triumphal conclusion that the sting of death has been removed (1 Cor. 15.55). Because Jesus, the Messiah, was raised from death to new life, the world necessarily looks different. Resurrection life is now seen as possible and has been witnessed. In their encounters with the risen Jesus, the disciples saw at first hand that God had brought Jesus to a new dimension of life over which death no longer had any authority (Wright, 2007, p. 68).

St Paul talks about Jesus' new life as first fruits from the dead (1 Cor. 15.20). This agricultural image is worth exploring a little. I live in farming country and every year the local farmers are relieved when they get the first crop of grass harvested in June. The farmers interpret a good first harvest as a sure sign that the rest of the year's crops will successfully appear towards the autumn. The June harvest, known locally as 'the first cut' (first fruits), is seen as a guarantee that the rest will follow. The ancient Jews clearly practised a similar agricultural pattern of first and second harvests. This is reflected in the development of two harvest festivals commanded in the Old Testament: the early grain harvest festival of Shavuot or Pentecost (first-fruits harvest) and the later festival of Succoth or Booths at the later harvest time (Exod. 34.18–23; Deut. 16.9–10, 13). Clearly, St Paul was familiar with the practice and he makes use of this imagery in his first letter to the Corinthians. Here he says that the resurrection of Jesus is like the first fruits from the dead, and this first human resurrection is a sure sign that other resurrections will, in due course, follow. The resurrection of Jesus, then, guarantees the possibility of resurrection for us.

The possibility of resurrection is a tremendous hope in which millions of Christians have put their trust down the ages. From the first Christians, whose stories are told in the Acts of the Apostles, to those living today, countless believers have implicitly trusted in the hope of new life beyond death. For many people their confidence in this hope has been so solid that, even in the face of persecution and martyrdom, they have not wavered. The resurrection of Jesus serves as a reminder that God's promises are to be trusted because, in Jesus, God shows that he can create a future out of the disappointment and reality of human death (Herbert, 2006, p. 94).

So the first reason for Christians to hope is that death is not the end: we have a resurrected future to look forward to and in which we can hope. This can serve as an encouragement to start thinking and talking about our own future death.

Some of us may wish for more detail concerning what the promised resurrection life will look like. Perhaps frustratingly, the Bible does not give many explicit details, but the glimpses it does reveal sound pretty good! For example, the Bible confidently teaches that life beyond death will be qualitatively different from what has gone before: that is to say, it will be better than this life. The book of Revelation depicts this new life as the city of God, which will be a place where there is no more death, mourning, crying or pain (Rev. 21.4). It will be a place where God will live with his people (21.3); where nothing impure will happen (21.27); and where all nations will walk by the light of God (21.24). Here the cross will not be a painful memory but a sign of splendour and honour, as Jesus, the lamb who was slain, will be a lamp shining light on all (21.23). This is a place of worship (4.10; 5.14; 7.11; 11.16) where we will see God and serve him (22.3–4). In this place we will be given new and glorious resurrection bodies that are imperishable and healed of all former pains and hurts (1 Cor.

15.42). Put succinctly, the Bible presents life beyond death as a place of glory and perfection, where it will be possible to experience the richness of human community, yet without the taint of sin (Proctor, 2012, p. 6).

It could be that resurrection life will be so qualitatively different from life as we know it that if we were presented with clear unambiguous details about it now, we simply would not have the conceptual tools to process the data. In the synoptic Gospels, this idea is captured in an encounter between Jesus and a group of Sadducees who did not believe in resurrection (Mark 12.18–27; Matt. 22.23–33; Luke 20.27–40). In answer to a question about how husbands and wives will relate to each other post-resurrection, Jesus replies: 'At the resurrection we're beyond marriage. As with the angels, all our ecstasies and intimacies then will be with God' (Matt. 22.30, The Message). Therefore, we may have to content ourselves now with the hints and clues in the Bible regarding what life beyond death will be like.

It may help to understand that the New Testament maintains that resurrection life does not just involve individual human beings: it is part of the new creation that God intends to bring about for the whole world. In the letter to the Romans, St Paul speaks of the entire creation eventually being liberated from its bondage to decay and brought into the glorious freedom of the children of God (Rom. 8.21). It is noteworthy that in the picture of resurrection life given in the book of Revelation, nature is also very much part of things. In the new city of God, the water of life is freely available to all (Rev. 21.6) and the tree of life flourishes (22.2). The original natural order depicted in the spoiled garden of Eden comes to fruition in the resurrection life. Human life beyond death, then, is part of something far bigger, for eventually God will make *all* things new (21.5). The fact that our individual death is part of the bigger and supremely hopeful picture may lend an air of assurance to some who wish to think about their own passing from this world.

Some Christians have found the following metaphor from the world of computing helpful in getting a firm hold on the idea that life beyond death will be infinitely better than life in the here and now. The late John Polkinghorne, theoretical physicist, theologian and Anglican priest, suggested that, at the resurrection, it will be as though God downloads our software on to his hardware and then gives us new hardware to run the software again (2002, p. 107). The idea here is that with God's hardware, life will be qualitatively and infinitely better than anything we know in the present. So a second reason for Christians to face the idea of death with some confidence is that faith tells us that life beyond death is something to which we can look forward.

Reflecting on the particular task that death performs for humanity may also reassure Christians wanting to think about their own death. If we were to ask ourselves what we under-stand as the purpose of death, I wonder what our answer might be? Many church funeral liturgies see death as the gateway to a fuller life with God (United Reformed Church, 1999). In this view, death fulfils a positive function. St Paul goes as far as saying that at a certain point in his life he came to see death as a gain to which he looked forward: 'For to me, living is Christ and dying is gain' (Phil. 1.21) and 'I desire to depart and be with Christ' (Phil. 1.23).

Similarly, the writer Rob Moll points out that, from a Christian perspective, death can be a mercy (2010, p. 26). Not only does it represent the final end of any afflictions we may have known in this life, it also serves as the entrance to life with God. Because of this, Moll says that death can even be beautiful. While not denying that death can be fearful – and, at times, ugly – Christian faith, for Moll, can transform death into a thing of beauty and purpose. He concedes, however, that death may never be easy to contemplate because it remains as mysterious to us as the resurrection.

Therefore, although we may be fearful of death or at least hesitant about it, when death is conceptualized as a door to life with God in all its fullness and richness, we may come to a place where we are more comfortable thinking about it.

A further encouraging thought that has built confidence

in Christians down the centuries is that we do not face death alone. In Jesus, God is with us in death. Indeed, the fact that God in Christ experienced human death is a very important part of Christianity's unique theology and appeal. To those unfamiliar with the Christian story, it is startling that we believe that, in the person of Jesus, God became a human being. In Jesus, God not only entered the world as we enter it – that is, he was born in the normal biological way – but he also went out of the world as we go out of it, by dying a human death. If we've been a Christian for some time, this core principle of our faith may have lost some of its radical force. In that case, it may be helpful to pause for a moment and re-engage with the awesome implications of the doctrine of the incarnation regarding the human experience of death. It is astonishing that God in Christ did not only walk with us along the sunny lanes of Galilee but also laid alongside us on the sunless shelf of the grave and beside us on the mortuary slab (Lloyd, 2020, p. 202). The foundational Christian belief of 'Emmanuel', God-is-with-us, is as relevant at the hour of our death as during all the hours of our life.

The confidence-inspiring thought here is that we can be enabled to face our own death because we know that Jesus was able to do it and has trodden the way before us. The seventeenth-century nonconformist Richard Baxter (1615–91) gave voice to this conviction in his famous hymn 'Lord, it belongs not to my care', a line from which reads: 'Christ leads me through no darker rooms than he went through before.' Significantly, Baxter notes that not only will Christ be with us in the dark rooms of death but he will also lead us *through* these rooms and onwards to new life. Assurance can grow as we remember that Jesus himself did not remain dead in the tomb in Jerusalem but rose to new life. As the words on Jesus' lips in Revelation read: I am ... the living one. I was dead, and see, I am alive for ever and ever; and I have the keys of Death and of Hades (Rev. 1.17–18). Some Christians have found that thinking and talking about their death has also given rise to thinking about their present life in a new and meaningful way.

Thinking about their death has also caused them to consider their priorities in life and what they want to do with the time they have left. The writer of Ecclesiastes encourages his readers to 'eat your food with gladness, and drink your wine with a joyful heart ... no one knows when their hour will come' (Eccles. 9.7, 12 NIV).

This may seem similar to Stoic philosophy, but in his letter to the Philippians St Paul provides a much more positive and Jesus-centred reason for taking hold of life with new fervour and enthusiasm. As much as he wanted to be beyond death in order to be with Jesus, Paul decided to pour himself out for those around him, even to the point of risking his life, so that they should know the love of God revealed in Jesus: 'Convinced of this, I know that I will remain, and I will continue with all of you for your progress and joy in the faith' (Phil. 1.25 NIV).

In contemplating death Paul had paradoxically found, or perhaps rediscovered, a reason for living. Karl Barth comments that Paul resolutely affirms Jesus Christ as his 'beyond', and this gives impetus to the compulsion to serve God with joy in his life here and now (1966, p. 118). Put colloquially, the thought of his own inevitable death had made Paul want to 'grab life with both hands'. So, strangely enough, to take Jesus at his word – to believe that he is the resurrection and the life and that whoever believes in him will live, even though they die – can release us from having to think about death for too long. Instead, we can focus our energies on living in the here and now.

Acquiring such an attitude may not come easily to everyone, and to be free from fear and to step out in life with fresh purpose may take courage. However, we must not underestimate another basic assertion of Christian faith, which is that we believe God will meet all our needs according to the riches of his glory in Christ Jesus (Phil. 4.19). In the Christian life, we are not alone either in death or life.

Summary

In this chapter I have argued that there are many reasons for Christians to feel confident in thinking about the prospect of their own death. Although this issue is a sensitive one that some people may find upsetting, we can be enabled to face the mystery of death with a measure of calm assurance. Christian faith clearly affirms that death is not the end, and life after death is portrayed as qualitatively better than life in this world. Additionally, death has a purpose: it can be viewed as the gateway to a fuller life with God. The thought that Jesus underwent death, and so stands in solidarity with us, can be a comforting one and we may even find that musing on our mortality provides new energy and savour to our mortal life.

The fact that death brings sorrow is not swept away by faith, and the potential need to grieve for ourselves is not ignored. The sheer disappointment that can be generated when thinking about our own death is not denied but can be transformed as we look to the future in hope and expectation.

The story of the two disciples walking to Emmaus after Jesus' crucifixion (Luke 24.13–35) is an exquisite illustration of how Christian faith can turn the defeat of death into the victory of God. When the stranger who begins to walk by the side of the disciples asks why they are so downcast, they articulate their disappointment so poignantly when they say, 'we *had* hoped' (Luke 24.21). As we know, instead of overthrowing the Roman occupying force and restoring Israel to its former glory, Jesus had been crucified and now lay dead in a tomb. Their hopes are crushed and their futures uncertain, but the stranger who is in fact the risen Jesus explains to them what recent events actually mean. Through the resurrection the power of death has been broken. As Jesus breaks bread at the table the disciples' eyes are opened and their hearts burn within them. With a risen Jesus, the future is suddenly shot through with hitherto unimagined possibilities. We, like them, look to the future armed with such hope, and find that we can dare to think about our own death.

3

Societal Attitudes to Talking About Death and Dying

Let's acknowledge again that talking about our own death can be difficult for some people. That's OK. It's definitely a sensitive subject and who would want to upset themselves thinking about such things? We know in our rational minds that death will come knocking on our door one day, but we seem to consign thoughts of it to the very back of our minds. We don't exactly deny that one day we will die, but we just seem to close our minds to the fact of our own mortality.

Death as a remote prospect

These days in the Western, developed world, we don't often have to think about the possibility of dying prematurely. We live in a part of the world where average life expectancy is around 83 years and many of us are now living beyond the age of 100.

In 1988, my great aunt received a birthday card from the Queen on the occasion of her 100th birthday, and she was the only person I knew who had received such an honour. More recently, the late Queen had to take on extra staff to help her send these cards as a result of the dramatic increase in the number of centenarians. The Department for Work and Pensions now has a seven-strong 'Centenarian Team' dedicated to keeping the information on Britain's oldest residents up to date (Bingham, 2014). In fact, between 2000 to 2010, the number of people over the age of 100 jumped by 70 per cent.

Of course, we might not all make it to 100, but increasingly it seems that it is becoming the norm for people to live until they are 90. A century ago, the average was nearer 50 years.

The reasons for such increased life expectancy among the world's wealthiest populations can be attributed to a number of factors. These include improvements in public health – for example, better sanitation and universal access to clean drinking water; improved nutrition; and advances in medicine. Vaccinations and antibiotics have greatly reduced deaths in childhood; health and safety in factories and other working environments has improved enormously and fewer people now smoke. The decline in the fertility rate, largely as a result of better female education and availability of contraception, has had a bearing on the statistics. This is because women survive longer if they have fewer children. And thankfully, the vast majority of children in the developed world are very likely to survive into adulthood.

All of this is good and stands in sharp contrast to the situation in many countries where life expectancy is considerably lower. But it does mean that we are somewhat removed from the necessity of thinking and talking about death as a matter of common course. Surely, death happens to very old people, we may think, not us.

Perhaps we are out of practice because we have the luxury of postponing such thoughts and now don't know how to do it. When we try to do this kind of thinking, we can become upset and find it difficult to access help, so we put it off.

Longevity at all costs

Being upset by the thought of death is, of course, very normal. Our natural inclination is to avoid death. The biological survival instinct is necessarily strong and, arguably, our most powerful driver. It has influenced the way human societies have developed to better organize themselves into groups that are more likely to find food and survive harsh conditions.

The survival instinct has driven advances in technology and medical science. Some would go so far as to argue that we all tend to see death as a medical failure, or at best a mistake. As a chaplain I have supported families who have been surprised and angry that the doctors were unable to save the life of their 90-something-year-old relative who had widespread irreversible cancer. Their view was that the system had failed them. They believed there should have been something that could have been done to prolong their relative's life and to postpone their death.

While I have complete sympathy for grieving families, it has always seemed to me that denying death as the natural end of a long life can be most unhelpful. In the first place, such an attitude may impede the family's ability to focus on the immediate needs of their relative, which will most likely be for calm emotions and gentle, steady support.

The dying person may well know that they are, in fact, dying, and to have this recognized by loved ones and professionals can bring profound relief. To be told by close family members 'Don't talk like that – you're going to get better soon' could obstruct important conversations that the dying person may want to have with their loved ones.

For example, the person dying may want to say goodbye to the family, to make sure they've made a will, sorted out their finances and 'got their house in order'. They may want to see particular people in order to complete unfinished emotional business: for example, there may be people they wish to forgive or people they want to see one last time so they can be reconciled with them. All this is denied to them if they're encouraged to buy into the myth that they're going to get better soon.

A death-denying attitude can also have a detrimental effect on family members that can last for months and years after the death. In particular, lack of preparedness for the death of a loved one is a risk factor for what clinicians call *complicated or disenfranchised grief*. This is when normal progression through bereavement is hampered and the grieving person finds it extremely difficult to move on (Read and Elliott, 2007).

The culture of death-denial is not helpful but it is a feature of Western society. The survival instinct is strong indeed. We are so used to this that we hardly notice it. There is now such an increased desire to avoid death and cling on to life at all costs that people are now making arrangements to have themselves cryogenically frozen after death and kept on ice until a future time when, they hope, medical science can revive them to give them a second shot at life on earth.

So it seems that talking about death and dying runs counter to the survival instinct and the increasing longevity-at-all-costs mentality that has seeped into our collective consciousness. Understanding that *we* may have such a mindset could be the first step towards changing. We can now consider whether we want to continue being in denial and avoiding the subject of death and dying or whether we want to start talking about the end of life.

Recent societal trends in talking about death

The attitude of longevity-at-all-costs that seems to have seeped into our collective consciousness has been a long time in the making. It is part of how society's attitudes to death have evolved.

During the twentieth century, it was often asserted that talking about death had become taboo in the UK. In everyday usage, of course, 'taboo' refers to something prohibited or forbidden by custom rather than by law. At its extreme, something that is taboo may be too terrible even to think about or, more commonly, something that is not mentioned in conversation (Walter, 1991, p. 91).

Recent statistics tend to suggest that talking about death is still taboo in the early twenty-first century. A 2016 ComRes survey showed that people are more comfortable talking about most things other than dying. Around 80 per cent of people in the survey were comfortable talking about immigration, politics, religion and money compared with only 64 per cent who felt comfortable talking about dying. Only sex scored lower as a comfortable topic of conversation, with 50 per cent of people feeling at ease talking about it (Figure 1).

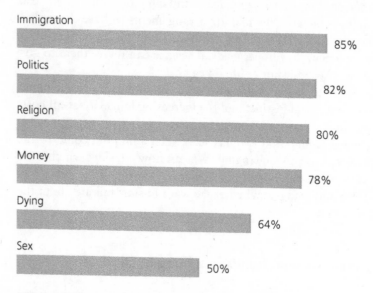

Figure 1: Topics people are comfortable talking about (ComRes, 2016)

Statistics on the way we prepare for our death also appear to reveal a degree of reticence in broaching these matters (Figure 2). About one-third of us have done things like written our wills, registered as organ donors or talked about our choices for a funeral. Even fewer – around a quarter of us – have talked about our end-of-life wishes and fewer than one in ten have written these wishes down. One-third of us have not engaged in anything to do with end-of-life preparations.

Some people believe that death became a taboo subject in the early part of the twentieth century when the modern age came into view. Victorian stylized mourning rituals were gradually abandoned and beliefs and moral values became varied and individualistic (Gorer, 1965, p. 110). In this new pluralistic

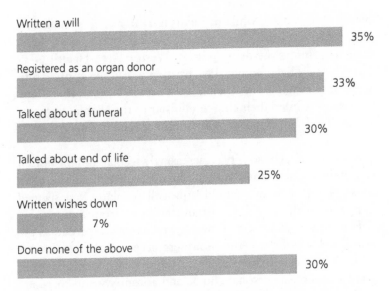

Figure 2: Percentage of people who have made end-of-life preparations (Statistics compiled by the Dying Matters campaign in 2014)

society, there was no agreed framework for a discourse about death.

In earlier times, when the UK was much more of a mono-culture, most people did the same thing at the time of a death, and people seemed to know what they were expected to do. Walter (2003) has suggested that to all intents and purposes there was an agreed 'community script' for dying, which included sending for the local Christian priest to perform the last rites at the home of the dying person.

In the twenty-first-century multicultural context, however, it may be deemed inappropriate or simply irrelevant to ask the local Christian priest to visit. Today we live in a more diverse society where people with different religious and philosoph-ical ideas live side by side, especially in urban areas. People of non-Christian faiths and philosophies will clearly want to follow their own religious customs. For example, there are specific words that Muslims are encouraged to recite before death (Ford, 2020), while in Judaism there are no specific last rites but it is considered important that everything possible be done to comfort the dying person (Weston Area Health NHS Trust, 2020). Even within the Christian world the approach to death varies. When I worked in the hospice, I found that many Christians wanted their church minister or the chaplain present at the death, but not every Christian felt this was necessary or desirable.

Furthermore, UK society is increasingly secular and the notion of nominal Christianity is much less prevalent. In times past, those people who we would now call secular often seemed happy to go along with Christian traditions around death.

For example, Christian funerals were largely regarded as the norm whether or not the mourners accepted the sentiments of faith expressed therein. These days, many secular people want to exercise personal choice and autonomy and there are more and more secular funerals taking place without a minister of any kind of religion. It is now not uncommon for family and friends to put a ceremony together themselves, reflecting their own particular perspective on life and death. Influenced, perhaps, by this trend, contemporary Christian funerals are gradually becoming more bespoke as mourners frequently offer input into the service by, for example, suggesting the inclusion of favourite poems and music and by being ready to give their personal reflections about the person who died. It would seem, then, at this point in time there is no clear route to follow as death approaches (Walker, 2020, p. 8).

At the same time, the increasing success of medical science, with its revolutionary advances in antibiotic therapy, transplant surgery, diagnostic techniques and preventative medicine, means that prolonging life, rather than preparing for death, has become the dominant medical model. Not only has prolonging life taken over from preparing for death but now, when death occurs, it no longer generally happens in the family home but in the clinical settings of hospitals and nursing homes.

Even within my own lifetime I have witnessed death becoming more removed from the family setting. The first dead body

I saw belonged to my gran. I was ten years old when she died in her own bed, which was in the front room (the parlour) of our family home. All her children were with her when she died. The next day, a coffin was brought to the house and set up on a sort of trestle arrangement in the parlour. My gran was placed in the coffin and there she stayed for a couple of days as various family members and neighbours came in to say their last good-byes and to sympathize and pray with the family. As a child I was included in all of this. I clearly remember standing at the side of the coffin with my mother, aunties and great-aunties, who were all reminiscing about my gran. And when I got upset the grown-ups comforted me and encouraged me to talk about my memories too.

In contrast to my experience, my daughter was in her twenties by the time she saw her first dead body; and it wasn't at home and it wasn't someone she knew. She saw her first dead body in the hospital where she was a medical student. Many of her non-medical contemporaries have still not seen a dead body, for death has become the province of healthcare professionals rather than family members.

Because, these days, most people die within healthcare settings, death has become somewhat removed from everyday experience and many are now largely ignorant of what death actually entails. Indeed, part of the inspiration for the modern hospice movement grew out of the perception that the UK had become a death-denying culture, or at least a death-ignorant one. Therefore the hospice movement sought to reclaim death as a natural phenomenon and societal norm, rather than something to be denied, not talked about and hidden away (Saunders, 2003, p. 28).

In spite of this, some commentators have noted in recent times that death is once again becoming something we *can* talk about (Zimmerman and Rodin, 2004). For example, no Sunday newspaper seems to be without at least one article discussing death, bereavement, hospices or funerals. Books and films on death and dying continue to proliferate (Walter, 1991). Just pause for a moment and – without thinking too hard – see how many films or books you can come up with that cover this topic. I gave myself one minute and came up with the following list:

- *The Bucket List*
- *Ghost*
- *Love Story*
- *My Sister's Keeper*
- *Four Weddings and a Funeral*
- *The Lovely Bones*
- *The Descendants*
- *The Fault in Our Stars*
- *Sleepless in Seattle*
- *The Hours*
- *Philadelphia*
- *P.S. I Love You*
- *Up!*
- *Rent*

So it seems clear that the film industry at least is addressing this subject. Add to this the number of television deaths you can witness in any given week, courtesy of the files of various fictional police detectives, including Inspectors Taggart, Lynley, Lewis, Stanhope, Gently and Barnaby, not to mention programmes such as *Law and Order UK*, *Broadchurch*, *Silent Witness*, *Waking the Dead*, *Sherlock* and *CSI*. With such a viewing diet you'd think we'd all be well informed about the mechanics of death and therefore well able to face the issues that it raises.

In reality, all this shows is that in some ways UK society is obsessed with melodramatic death but the reality of 'ordinary' death and dying is less prominently discussed. So we may not learn much from the sensationalist world of television and film that would help us approach the task of talking about our own death. What these media deal with is the drama of death rather than the issues it raises. However, with a little imagination, dramas about death could be used as a way into discussing all manner of end-of-life issues.

So does society help us talk about *our* death? I think the answer is yes and no. Some aspects of society are death-denying and death-ignorant. However, if we are beginning to talk about death again, at least in film and on television, then perhaps that's a start.

Healthcare professionals' attitudes to talking about death

One group within society that does have experience of death is healthcare professionals, and their attitudes to talking openly about death are most illuminating. Within the UK healthcare community, we are currently witnessing a more positive view of the value of talking openly about death and dying. This is particularly so when healthcare professionals deal with people who are approaching the end of their lives. Even in this context, in times past doctors and nurses sometimes deemed it best to withhold a terminal diagnosis from their patients. They judged that this was best all round. The patient would then not lose hope or cause a scene because they could rest assured that 'everything possible was being done'. The prevailing wisdom was that certain things were better left unsaid. Nowadays, withholding information from patients is considered unethical. At the very least, healthcare professionals are obliged to make it clear when further medical treatments would be futile.

And it's not just about telling people that there are no more treatments that will prolong their lives. In this day and age, doctors and nurses concern themselves with wider issues around death. It is now broadly recognized that there are other issues to take into account when making decisions about the end of one's life. The moral beliefs and values of the dying person are seen as important parts of any discussion about the patient's end-of-life wishes. This is sometimes called the bio-ethical approach. We may think of it as taking a more philosophical approach to decision-making rather than an exclusively medical one.

These days, when discussing the appropriateness of certain medical treatments for people approaching the end of their lives, doctors and nurses include considerations of the patient's philosophical and spiritual wishes. An example of this is whether the side effects of an offered treatment would greatly outweigh the benefits.

Let's imagine ourselves in such a situation. Let's say you had terminal cancer, but also a serious heart condition. The cardiologists have offered you major surgery that might help your heart but couldn't cure your cancer. It would be a major operation involving a lot of risk and several months of recovery. You'd have quite a lot to think about before consenting to surgery. Questions concerning quality of life in your remaining time could be intensely relevant.

Healthcare professionals taking a bio-ethical approach would encourage you to reach a decision on grounds other than whether a medical treatment is technically possible and available. They'd encourage you to consider your quality of life post-surgery in your limited time. They might encourage you to think about how you want to spend your remaining time and whether such surgery would impede any of your ambitions. Some people would decide to decline further treatment because they would see time spent recovering from surgery as a painful distraction from the kind of things they'd rather be doing. For them, further treatment (not just surgery) would not only be viewed as futile, in that it would not be curative, but would also be robbing them of time that could be spent doing non-medical things.

On the other hand, striving for life at all costs and availing themselves of all medical interventions could be very important for some people. For such individuals, it would be imperative to opt for any and all medical procedures, even if the chances of success were slim or in some way life-limiting. Making every effort to preserve life could be bound up with views about the meaning and purpose of life, and within such a view the option of further treatment could represent a great source of hope. Discussing these sorts of options with doctors and nurses would include much more than purely medical matters.

But end-of-life matters are not only being aired during encounters between healthcare professionals and those coming towards the end of their lives. Recent years have seen an increasing trend for various clinical specialities to offer patients the opportunity to talk about end-of-life planning even though they may not yet be approaching the end of their lives. So if you have certain medical conditions, you might be asked about whether you want to talk about your end-of-life plans while you are attending a dialysis unit or Chronic Obstructive Pulmonary Disease (COPD) clinic; or while you are a patient on a general medical or elderly care ward of an acute hospital or in the intensive care unit. Increasingly, senior-citizen centres and care homes are also offering end-of-life planning conversations (Gutheil and Heyman, 2005).

One example of this kind of thing is a scheme in Glasgow among patients with heart failure who have been identified as nearing the end of their lives (Marie Curie, 2011). This scheme, run by the British Heart Foundation and Marie Curie, facilitates conversations about where and how patients want to be cared for at the end of their lives. Interestingly, this was set up in response to some research carried out by the Parliamentary and Health Service Ombudsman (2015), which expressed the view that end-of-life care for non-cancer patients could be greatly improved by greater knowledge of patient needs and wishes at the end of their lives (Parliamentary and Health Service Ombudsman, 2015).

Being offered the opportunity to talk about our death in response to different kinds of medical encounters, and not only during palliative-care-type conversations, is to my mind a really helpful development. It can perhaps begin to normalize the notion of talking about end-of-life matters while we are still in the midst of life.

Moreover, as this kind of work has developed in recent years, healthcare professionals are acquiring skills to be able to do this competently and sensitively. Nowadays, doctors and nurses routinely undergo training in communication skills to aid them in talking to us about this. It is fair to say that training in specific end-of-life communication skills varies across the country (Munday, Petrova and Dale, 2009). Some hospital staff have reported feeling ill-equipped to initiate and undertake end-of-life conversations in a way that would not cause distress to patients (Thompson-Hill and colleagues, 2009). Happily, there are also successful examples of doctors and nurses feeling well equipped and confident to tackle such work with patients in a direct and open way (Field, Finucane and Oxenham, 2013). As these skills are accrued over time and become more embedded in medical and nursing training, we can expect to see increasing levels of confidence among our doctors and nurses when approaching us to open discussions about end-of-life care.

Churches talking about death and dying

In Chapter 2, I asserted that Christian faith has much to say about death and dying. It is unclear, however, how much is actually said about death and dying within churches. When funerals are conducted in churches, and during the course of planning a funeral, the subject of the death of the person for whom the funeral is being held can hardly be avoided. In addition, Christian belief regarding life and death will be rehearsed through Bible readings and prayers said within the service. Bereavement care will be much in evidence on the day of the funeral, and this is often sensitively practised by church communities in the coming days, weeks and months. On the whole, I would like to think that churches do this sort of thing pretty well.

It must also be acknowledged that some churches excel at ministry around the time of a death. As people approach death, ministers and pastoral carers often make visits to them at their home or place of care, which might, for example, be a hospital, hospice or nursing home. At this point comfort may be offered through prayer ministry, administration of the sacraments or simple conversation and companionship. Matters relating to death may or may not be raised by the person being visited, but nevertheless the church gets involved in the death experience. These sorts of encounters can be profound and beautiful, and some turn out to be deep encounters with God that bless both the church visitor and the dying person. So I would argue that the church does not shy away from supporting people through death.

What is less certain, however, is how much death and dying *in general* is discussed within the church community and as part of the rhythm of the church's life. I would question whether churches preach much about death and dying outside of the context of funerals. Many clergy feel ill-equipped to do this sort of work, as they believe they do not possess the necessary pastoral skills or theological knowledge. Some have reported a sense of uncertainty about the precise nature of resurrection hope, making them cautious about leading others through this territory with authority and integrity (Collicutt, 2019). Others are of the opinion that people would find it morbid to be asked to reflect on end-of-life matters before they absolutely have to. Furthermore, it is argued, the church's task is rather to help people focus on life rather than death, because Christians are, after all, 'Easter People' (Townshend, 2018).

A great appetite for talking about end-of-life matters among churchgoers has yet to be determined. Sometimes people talk to their ministers about what they'd like to happen at their funeral. I have had several conversations with people who have wanted to tell me which hymns they'd like at their funeral or which church they'd like their funeral to take place in, or whether or not they'd like me to preside at the service. On the whole, these people are elderly or in poor health, but occasionally a younger person has broached the subject with me, quite often during the refreshments after a funeral.

Perhaps matters relating to our own death seem easier to discuss when we've just been in the same room as a friend's or relative's coffin. Attending a funeral can act as our own personal prompt to thinking about death. However, funerals usually talk about the person who has died and not about any wider issues related to death and dying. Moreover, no church has yet reported a groundswell of people asking the church to help them talk about end-of-life matters while they are still in the midst of life.

So it would seem that 'death-talk' is still not routine in church circles. Contrast this with the way many churches regularly run courses preparing people for other significant life events, such as marriage, baptism and church membership. Yet it is not commonplace for churches to run preparation-for-death courses, or even courses on the theology of death and dying.

A growing number of resources are becoming available for church use. For example, the Diocese of Oxford has produced an excellent death-preparation course (Diocese of Oxford, 2020). Similarly, the 'Grave Talk' material produced by the Church of England provides an almost step-by-step guide on how to organize an event at which people can talk about end-of-life matters in a relaxed and supportive setting (Millar, 2015). Clearly such courses and events are springing up, but the extent of the take-up of these initiatives is at best patchy and not yet widespread. I have read about such events taking place but in practice I've never found one being offered in a church near me.

It is my hope that this will change in the coming years and that churches will build on such new initiatives to become places where death and dying can be openly discussed for the benefit of all. I hope that clergy and church members will acquire both the skills and wisdom required to help people learn how to die. In the medieval Christian world a broad tradition of writing and reflecting on death and dying developed, which was known as 'the art of dying' (or *Ars moriendi*) movement (Shinners, 1997). Perhaps we are witnessing the first stages of such a movement in the Church of today.

Summary

We've seen that talking about death and dying can be difficult and that in many ways contemporary culture in the UK does not encourage it, so we are rather unsure how to go about it. But we've also seen that there are signs that these attitudes are changing.

4

Some Benefits of Talking About Death and Dying

We've looked at some of the reasons we might find it difficult to think or talk about our own death, as it's a sensitive and upsetting subject for some people. We've also seen that in some ways we see our own death as rather a remote concept, something that happens to other people – not us. We've also noted that at this point in Western society, death usually happens within the safe confines of a medical facility of some sort. So surely death need not concern us, at least for the time being. After all, we'd much rather concentrate on prolonging life.

We've seen too how death is still somewhat taboo in our culture and that we'd rather talk about almost anything else than death. We don't mind vicariously experiencing sensational death through books, television and film – indeed, I confess I enjoy the occasional murder mystery myself!

As we've seen, doctors and nurses in the past didn't always encourage open discussion of death with their patients, so this sometimes acted as a barrier to the exploration of end-of-life matters. We've been thankful, though, that there's now a growing willingness among healthcare professionals to help us talk about our deaths. We've recognized that this work is difficult for them too but that they are working on acquiring the skills and expertise to carry it out.

We've seen that, outside of funerals, death and dying are not much discussed within churches, but this situation may be changing now there are a number of resources being produced that could help churches promote open discussion of the issues around death. Moreover, these sorts of resources could be offered as part of the normal diet of church courses and discussions, albeit such practice is not yet widespread.

We've also seen that, happily, we may now be witnessing the first stages of a cultural shift in both the secular and Christian world in which there is more willingness to talk about death and dying. It remains true, however, that talking about death and dying can be difficult and that, to some extent, UK contemporary culture – including the culture within churches – seems somewhat reluctant to embrace death as a normal topic of conversation.

Having seen that there are still many barriers to talking about death and dying and that this can be a difficult task to undertake, we may wonder whether we should attempt to do it. We may find ourselves asking whether there are actually any benefits to taking on such a difficult assignment. Put another way, if talking about death and dying is so difficult, why should we do it? Or we may ask 'What's in it for me?' In this chapter I will point to several benefits of discussing death and dying. Some of these benefits are practical and pragmatic, whereas others are more concerned with our well-being, including our relationship with God.

A spiritual experience

I have often found it to be the case that when people *do* talk about death and dying it turns out to be a deeply spiritual experience for them. This has been true regardless of whether people identify as having a defined faith. For example, I was once asked to talk with a hospice patient called Carys about her funeral wishes. (Note that all names have been changed for anonymity. Some 'people' are combinations of various folk I have met. The only real names used are my daughter Jessica, who gives her consent, and my dead cousin Viv, who would be thrilled and somewhat amazed to appear in a book.)

Carys was previously unknown to me: she had never attended a chapel service, requested bedside prayers or availed herself of the chaplaincy service in any way before, but this particular day she'd requested a talk with a chaplain about her funeral. I'll never forget the ultra-flippant and provocative manner in which she opened the conversation. No sooner had I sat down by her bed and told her my name than she proclaimed that, ideally, she'd like to have a Viking funeral in which her remains would be set fire to on a boat on the local canal, and she wanted to talk to me about how to arrange that. I can't remember what I said in reply but I'm sure my face eloquently conveyed my sense of shock and anxiety that she might actually mean what she said. This tension was broken by Carys who, taking one look at my face, laughed heartily and said: 'I bet that's a first for you, Rev. Don't worry, I won't really do that 'cos it'd be a waste of a bloody good boat.'

As I relaxed and our conversation moved into more realistic territory, I discovered that what Carys really wanted was someone to listen to her as she reflected on her life so far and tried to make sense of what it all meant. One theme that emerged from our conversation was her profound sense of thankfulness for her son, now grown up. Carys was emphatically glad that he (whom she had brought up on her own) had turned out to be a very well-adjusted young adult. He was doing a job that was fulfilling and secure and had just bought his own property. In Carys's view this made him 'properly independent' and she felt a certain sense of relief that she could go to her grave knowing he would be able to deal with whatever life sent his way. Moreover, Carys had a very positive relationship with her son and was grateful that she had already been able to have some conversations with him about the fact that death was not so far off for her now, and so she wanted him to know beyond doubt how much she loved him and how very proud she was of the person he'd become.

I suggested it sounded like she'd started to do her leave-taking of those she was close to and I asked whether that had been a helpful thing to do. She said it had brought her a kind of peace in her heart and that there was in fact no one else she needed to see, as her parents, brothers and sister had all died. She then went on to speak at some length of her happy childhood in South Wales and how much life in general had changed since the 1950s. At one point in this trip down memory lane, Carys paused, lowered her voice and said that her only regret was that she'd die before getting to see any grandchildren. She commented that her own childhood had been so full of people – brothers, sisters, aunts, uncles, cousins and grandparents – and now, at the end, there was just herself and her son. She said she bet I thought that meant something in the great scheme of things, but for her she was content to just be part of the universe both now and after death.

I felt very blessed by my conversation with Carys. I would go so far as to say it felt as if I'd been on holy ground as she shared her most personal thoughts and feelings about life, death and her place in the universe. For me this resonated with the many other conversations about death I've had over the years with all sorts of people, conversations that have often afforded me the opportunity to draw close to the other person's idea of meaning and values; to how they make sense of the world. Indeed, talking about death and dying can be a time when people engage with the deepest parts of themselves – that is, their spirituality.

As a former hospice chaplain, you would perhaps expect me to say that! I believe it is both good and necessary for human beings to sometimes be in touch with their souls or their spirituality, whatever that may mean to them. What do I mean by being 'in touch with our souls or spirituality'? I mean recognizing that part of us which is concerned with questions of meaning and purpose and the essence of what it means to be human (Kearney, 1990). For Christians, of course, this means being in touch with God and our faith in him. However, it seems important to acknowledge that such spirituality issues are relevant in the wider society too, and this may or may not include religion (Cobb, 2005, p. 40). Therefore, whatever a person's faith perspective, talking about the end of life can be a deeply spiritual matter, and I firmly believe that such discussion can be life-enhancing.

It is interesting to see a similar viewpoint reflected in recent developments within the secular world of healthcare. Modern healthcare, like most of Western culture, has been substantially shaped by rationalism and science (Russell, 1946, p. 491). However, as noted in Chapter 3, these days when doctors and nurses talk to people about end-of-life matters, they often widen the discussion to include more philosophical considerations, such as people's beliefs and values. Furthermore, the Gold Standards Framework (GSF), an initiative that aims to improve the quality of care for all people nearing the end of their lives, states that consideration of such issues can have the potential to enhance people's inner life, sense of optimism, autonomy, control and hope – and thus improve their quality of life (Gold Standards Framework, 2016). So even within the predominantly scientific paradigm of healthcare, which tends to frame the world in terms of problems that can be solved, a place for psycho-social-spiritual patient needs, in addition to medical goals, is valued (Walker, 2016, p. 197).

A sense of meaning and purpose here and now

It would seem, then, that talking about end-of-life matters in all its breadth and complexity has much support. For the Christian, of course, taking such an approach has a specific significance. Thinking about the end of our lives and what comes after can become an opportunity to go on a journey into wholeness with the God who made us, loves us and calls us into his eternity (Parker, Fraser and Rivers, 2003, p. 6). A fundamental tenet of Christian belief is that God created humans differently from all other beings, with a purpose that flows from our unique relationship with the immortal God. In the Genesis accounts of the creation of Adam and Eve, humans are the only creatures said to be made in God's image (Gen. 1.26), the only creatures into whom God breathes in order to create life (Gen. 2.7), and the only creatures to be given the task of stewardship of the world (1.28 and 2.18). Thus Christians regard themselves as physical beings infused with life by God and made in his image, and created for relationship with him, with one another and with the world. John Wesley, the founder of Methodism, viewed humanity as a balanced, harmonious organism designed for immortality (Ott, 1989). For the Christian, then, talking about death and dying can be an opportunity to engage with the wonderful and complex mixture of all that we are. In contemplating the eternal perspective, we could find an opportunity to apprehend afresh our place within God's great scheme of things. Perhaps we will discover that not only are we fearfully and wonderfully made (Ps. 139.14) but also there is a meaning to our existence and a purpose to our lives here and now.

This is well illustrated by an encounter I had with a young man called Delarno who had a traumatic brush with the reality that we are all but a hair's breadth away from death (United Reformed Church, 1999), which led him to re-evaluate his whole approach to life and to God. I first encountered Delarno when he phoned me to ask whether he would be allowed to come to my church service on Sunday. I replied that of course he would be, as everyone is welcome and we are delighted to see new faces. There was a pause on the end of the line and then Delarno explained that in fact he was not 'a new face' because he used to come to our church when he was a child. In those days he came every week with his grandma, who had now died. I said this made no difference and that I and the church family would look forward to welcoming him back. I went on to ask whether something had prompted his desire to come back to church. At this point Delarno became rather emotional and said that his little girl had recently been admitted to hospital and for a while her life had hung in the balance. I said a few sympathetic and encouraging words to give him time to recover, and when he got his emotions under control he told me his daughter was fine now – and then he paused again. I let the silence fall between us for a few moments and then I prompted him to go on, asking him whether there was something else. At this point Delarno began to speak quite quickly and loudly, saying:

> OK, yeah, but the thing is I prayed for her to get better. I've not prayed for years and I didn't know if God would be interested in listening to me anymore. I mean, I haven't spoken to him in years and I've not been a very good dad. You know, I've not been that involved in my little girl's life. But anyway I prayed in secret, like, and I just want to come to church on Sunday to thank God for saving her and for reminding me what the really important things are.

I thanked him for telling me his story and said I felt that coming to church on Sunday to say thank you to God would be a very appropriate thing to do. So I warmly encouraged him to come along and assured him that, as he may have remembered, there's always some time in our service when you can thank God for his goodness to you. On the following Sunday, Delarno came to the morning service and, sure enough, some of the old timers recognized him and welcomed him with open arms, both metaphorically and literally (it was a very tactile kind of church). They also told him that the evening service might interest him as it was 'more lively' than the morning one and more people of his age group went to that.

After that first Sunday, Delarno started coming to church regularly: first to morning service and then to the evening one, where he made friends with several people, started to play drums in the worship band and joined a home group, where he developed his growing Christian faith. One wonderful evening, at Testimony Time, he asked me if he could say his public thank you to God, not only for saving his daughter's life but for bringing him back to church and for helping him to find better ways of being involved in his little girl's life. So thinking about death and dying led this young man to consider many things in his life, not least his relationship with God and with those who were of utmost significance to him.

Practical benefits: planning for the future

Talking more openly about death and dying may not be about spirituality and faith exclusively. Some people may want to discuss more down-to-earth matters related to the end of life, such as financial planning for the future, making a will or talking about the kind of care they would like to have at the end of their lives. This is sometimes referred to as 'putting your house in order', and these issues can be just as important to Christians as to others. For some, this kind of practical thinking brings a sense of closure, as they feel they have articulated their own wants and desires. Furthermore, some people find giving directions to their loved ones about what they want to happen enables them to express care for the people they will be leaving behind. In helping to make practical arrangements about themselves, they feel they have alleviated some future potential worries for their loved ones, and this can bring a measure of peace of mind.

One expression of making practical arrangements regarding end-of-life matters that has been on the increase in recent years is that of planning for one's own funeral. Many people from all sorts of backgrounds and faith perspectives seem to feel this is a good way to ensure that their loved ones are spared the worry of planning and paying for their funeral at a time when they may be enveloped in the chaos of grief. Indeed, about one-fifth of all UK funerals are now paid for in advance via pre-paid funeral plans (Money Saving Expert, 2020).

Others may want to take a wider anticipatory planning approach by starting to think about not only what they want to happen after they die but also what might be important to them before they do. This may include thinking pragmatically about the kind of care they would like to receive as they approach the end of life. The great benefit of talking about such matters is the potential to influence what actually happens at the end.

One person's ideal way to spend their last days may be very different from someone else's. For example, I would like to be cared for at home, if possible, within a 'normal' family routine and atmosphere. I would welcome frequent visits from friends and family and would be quite happy with carers coming to the house to supplement and support the care that my family could give. By contrast, my husband's priority is privacy: he would want visiting strictly controlled. Now that we have talked about these things, our family knows what we each would, ideally, want and so can ultimately make arrangements to support our wishes. Had we not spoken up, our family would, I'm sure, have done what they *thought* we wanted, but at best they would have been guessing. People can only know what others want if they make their wishes known. Moreover, from a personal perspective I feel that open communication about this has meant I have been able to share something of great significance with those closest to me, and exercise a degree of agency over what will happen to me at the end.

Palliative care has long understood this and has championed an approach to healthcare that highly values and promotes personal autonomy and encourages people to make their own choices about their lives and health (Saunders, 1978, p. 35; National Institute for Clinical Excellence, 2004). Within this understanding, the notion of a good death would be one in which the patient had made their own choices about their last days and months and in which these choices had been heard and acted on. Conversely, a bad death would be one where a person exercised no autonomy and their wishes were unknown (Walter, 2003).

Whether or not we buy into the notion of good and bad deaths, it is clear that one way of influencing what happens to us at the end of our lives is to make our wishes and preferences known. One really important factor here is timing. The point along our life trajectory at which we choose to talk about the end of our life could have a bearing on whether our wishes are carried out. If we don't grasp this nettle, if we keep putting it off 'until something happens', we run the risk of leaving it until it's too late.

For example, many conversations on the topic of the end of life currently occur during an acute hospital admission. Usually, by this time there may have been a serious deterioration in the person's condition – that is, they are approaching the terminal phase of their life. At this point, the dying person may be too ill to take an active part in a discussion about their end-of-life preferences and wishes. If this is the case, it will then limit the extent to which such a conversation is possible and the person's voice gets heard. This will not be the easiest time to make informed choices about future desired care. If we leave it too late, our end-of-life care conversations may be of poor quality. Clearly, there are practical benefits to talking about our views on dying while we are in good health.

Increasing life expectancy is another reason to give practical attention to what we want to happen at the end of our lives. A previous generation did not have the same need to make plans for very old age because on the whole they died before that became an issue. Now, as people are living longer, they will probably need some level of supportive care in their later years. At some point the focus of that care will naturally turn towards end-of-life care. Therefore, if we want to exert some influence over what happens to us in extreme old age it would be a good idea to start thinking about this now. To that end, there is an increasing number of schemes to help patients and recipients of social care take control of their end-of-life wishes. For instance:

- In one hospital, elderly patients undergoing surgery are offered an information session about Advance Care Planning (Grimaldo and colleagues, 2001).
- In another hospital, cancer patients undergoing chemotherapy are offered a highly structured one-to-one Advance Care Planning intervention (Jones and colleagues, 2011).
- Many nursing homes now assist residents to express their wishes regarding end-of-life care.

Of course, such schemes include only those in hospital or those with illnesses who live in nursing homes. However, there is nothing to stop those of us who are currently healthy and in the midst of life from making a start in talking about death and dying.

Summary

We have seen that there are several benefits to talking about death and dying. This provides an opportunity for spiritual encounter: perhaps to grow in your faith and your relationship with God or at least to be in touch with the very deepest parts of yourself. Dealing with more practical matters, such as funeral planning or thinking about financial provision for those left behind, means that such issues can be discussed openly and dealt with in an efficient manner. Thinking pragmatically, it can be seen that this can make it easier for loved ones when the time comes. This may also have the benefit of providing the dying person with a certain peace of mind and may even afford an opportunity to interact with loved ones in a new and deep way. Furthermore, talking about death and dying opens up the possibility of exercising agency and the chance to influence what actually happens at the end.

5

Examples of People Talking About Death and Dying

In the last chapter I argued that openly talking about death and dying has certain benefits, such as providing an opportunity to focus on making practical arrangements for ourselves and our loved ones, while other gains concern our spiritual life. Of course, along the way it has also been acknowledged that talking about our own death can be difficult. However, I am convinced that this is not an impossible task; many people have already done this successfully and not everyone finds it difficult anyway.

It has been my privilege to journey alongside people who have talked about their views on their own death to their family and friends. I met some of these people when they were hospice patients and others when I served as a local church minister. I believe we can learn a lot from how others have approached this and I therefore share some of their stories in this chapter. It is my hope that reading about others' experience will provide some pointers as to how to approach this task, in addition to providing encouragement to follow their examples.

In my career as a hospice chaplain I talked with many people about their hopes and fears concerning the end of their lives. However, not everyone was focused on this issue. You may find it surprising, perhaps, that some hospice patients of my acquaintance – that is, those living with a terminal diagnosis and a relatively short prognosis – did not talk much to anyone about their oncoming deaths. Two such people were Henry and Mick, whose stories I tell below. The fact that they had not really talked much about the end of their lives came to light when hospice staff asked them where they wanted to be cared for at the end. These two men approached this subject from very different angles.

Henry's story

Henry attended the day hospice once a week, where he was very much part of the gang. He got great pleasure out of the general-knowledge quiz and often came to chapel for our service of Christian worship. He was an older gentleman who had lived through the Second World War, including the horrors of a Japanese prisoner-of-war camp. Although he never talked in detail about his experiences in Burma, he did talk about how hard it had been to readjust to civilian life back in England in the late 1940s. All in all, Henry came across as a thoughtful, gentle man. I often wondered whether his wartime years had contributed to his wistful nature or whether he had always been like that.

I spoke to Henry about death and dying when he had been admitted to the in-patient unit at the hospice. The doctors were making various assessments and trying out different support-ive drug regimes to ease his difficulties, and as this would take about a week, he'd come to stay in the hospice for that time. While he was there, I visited him daily and we talked about whatever he felt like talking about. When I asked him if he'd made any plans about where he wanted to spend his last days, he had an interesting observation to make. Henry said that until one of the nurses had broached this subject with him earlier that day, he'd not given it much thought. Then he said:

> I mean you tend to think you'd like to die at home, but in my own home, now with things being as they are, it wouldn't be very practical. So I've had to think again. I've made arrange-ments to come here [the hospice] and I feel it's really the right thing to do for our Marjorie. She's too old and poorly herself to cope with me at the end. It wouldn't be fair. I'm quite con-

tent about it actually, Sue, and so is she. So you'll be seeing some more of me yet.

So for Henry, this rather thoughtful man, it was one of the hospice nurses who had prompted him to consider 'making arrangements'. He did not seem to find talking about the end of his life traumatic in any way. In fact, he just accepted the opportunity to think about things and to make his wishes known, and found that this brought him some peace of mind. Being asked directly about matters concerning the end of his life, Henry was very able to think things through and put plans in place, and be at ease about it. Significantly, Henry did this 'work' while he was still in a fit state to do so. At the time, he was fully conscious and not in any great physical distress, so was perfectly able to become a co-creator of his future care and to take account of his family situation. Both Henry's needs and his wife's were considered and addressed to the contentment of both.

Interestingly, this quiet, pensive man who was already living with a terminal illness and a limited life expectancy had not given his end-of-life arrangements much thought until the hospice nurse brought the subject up. For someone in Henry's position, we might have expected that making plans for the end would have acquired a sense of urgency. However, he had needed prompting to think about practicalities.

Mick's story

Mick was a hospice patient who did not instantly warm to the idea of talking about the end of his life. Unlike Henry, Mick found such a prospect much less positive, and even rather shocking. This came to light one afternoon in the day hospice when there'd been a group discussion with patients about the possibility of recording their end-of-life wishes in a new document. The nurses had then followed this up by approaching individual patients to see whether they'd like a one-to-one discussion and some help filling in the relevant forms. Because Mick had been a bit upset when a nurse had tried to talk to him about this, she then asked me to see if he would like a chat to help clarify the situation.

As soon as we got talking, I could see that Mick had been disturbed by the encounter with the nurse. He looked troubled and sad. I asked him to tell me what had happened. Apparently, the nurse had approached him to see whether he wanted 'help filling in the form so he could sign it'. Mick said that had stopped him in his tracks, as he was sure he was not ready to sign any kind of form and he certainly did not want to be rushed into it. I asked him to try and say why he felt that way. He replied, 'Well, you've got to let it sink in, yeah? 'Cos when the nurse wanted to talk to me, well, I just hung back and I just, you know, couldn't get me head round it proper.'

In fact, Mick went on to document his end-of-life wishes in detail a few weeks later. He just needed time to process the whole idea that this was actually happening to him. As he talked it through with me, he was able to articulate a particular concern he had regarding the end of his life, one that he had never told anyone. He had a fear of dying at home and being carried out in a body bag, with all the neighbours looking on. For this reason, Mick definitely did not want to die at home. The thought of this really unsettled him, and although it was undoubtedly hard for him to say this out loud, once he'd been able to voice his fears with me he felt more in control. After a few days, Mick felt able to go back to the nurse who had originally approached him to record that he did not want to die at home.

Equally importantly, this process helped him to talk to his family about his wishes. Mick said that he was able to use the hospice end-of-life plan document as a way into a conversation with his family. Clearly, this was a very sensitive subject for him and I could imagine his agony at trying to broach it from scratch. Instead of this agony, though, Mick was able to open a conversation with his family by showing them the end-of-life plan he'd written at the hospice.

If Mick had not told anyone how he felt about dying at home, in the fullness of time his worst fear may indeed have come to pass. So for Mick, although it was difficult, talking about his end-of-life wishes proved to be a very effective tool in helping him achieve his desires. Furthermore, if Mick had not been made aware that talking about his end-of-life wishes was possible, I wonder whether he would have actually verbalized his particular concern. As it was, he was enabled to face his fears and make some plans to alleviate them. The notion of talking openly about death and dying may have been new to his family too, and so Mick may have been the agent of their education and learning.

The next two examples are women, at very different stages of life, who were members of my church. Both of them wanted to tell me about the recent conversations they had had about death and dying.

Mary's story

Mary was a member of my church whom I often visited at her home. Now in her eighties she lived alone, as her husband had died a few years earlier and her children had long since flown the nest: some to Birmingham, the nearest big city, and one to Canada. Mary had been a regular churchgoer all her life and very much part of our church family. Over the years she'd served faithfully in many roles, including Sunday School leader, community-café cook, prayer-group member, toddler-group founder and latterly foodbank organizer. Church attendance was becoming increasingly difficult for her as a result of the onset of various illnesses, aches and pains. She seemed to age all of a sudden, so she came out less and less and I visited her at home more and more.

The thing I recall most about Mary was that she was a great knitter. Whenever I called in to see her, she was clacking away with her needles, making someone in the family a new cardigan, hat or scarf. One afternoon, she made a pair of red mittens for me because, as she put it, 'I had a bit of yarn left over and I noticed that when you hold my hands to pray, yours are always cold.' I still have the mittens and when I put them on I get warm hands and a nice memory of a lovely lady.

When Mary told me about how she'd recently been prompted to think about the inevitability of her death, she did so in a very matter-of-fact manner one afternoon in her sitting room when, as usual, she was knitting as we talked. Mary told me that when she had recently been to see her GP to review her regular medications, he had asked her what she wanted to happen to her at the end of her life. She was a bit surprised when he said this because it had happened in the middle of a general chat about how she was managing. Knitting away, Mary described their conversation:

He [the doctor] just came out with it, like. He says to me, 'Mary, where do you want to go if you die?' So I says, 'The hospice please where my Bill died or, at a pinch, the hospital as I don't really want to be on my own', and he says, 'OK. Now I've got to ask you something else as well. Do you want to be resuscitated?' And I says, 'No thanks, Doctor. I know the score and I'll be all right.' So that's how it all came about.

I asked Mary how she felt about having that chat with the doctor when they talked about these serious matters, and this was her reply: 'He was very good about it, you know. I felt, well, relief 'cos now I'd got somewhere to go.' When I enquired whether she'd told her children about this, she said she had and that they'd encouraged her to tell me too, as they thought the church would be very much involved when the time came. For my part, I went on to share this information with the church leadership team (with Mary's permission, of course), thinking that the more people knew of her wishes the better we'd be able to support her.

Mary was not a hospice patient, neither was she living with a terminal diagnosis; she was just an ordinary member of the community getting on with her everyday life who took the opportunity to think about what she wanted to happen at the end. Significantly, Mary made her wishes fairly widely known: she not only shared them with her children but also with others who might have an impact on the care she would receive – that is, her GP and the church, who would be able to be alongside her at the end.

Rachel's story

Rachel, a young church member, told me that she'd recently talked to her husband about death and dying almost in the same breath that she told me she was pregnant. Yes, I *did* say 'pregnant'! At 30 years of age, Rachel was expecting her first baby and was nearly bursting with excitement as she showed me round the spare room she'd recently redecorated as a nursery, complete with a home-made mobile of cute-looking sheep hanging over the very smart new cot. I'd taken the wedding of Rachel and Dave the previous year and it was a great pleasure to share their joy as they waited for this new family member to make their entrance.

While I was admiring the décor of the nursery and reminiscing about how I'd revelled in *my* time as a mother of young children, Rachel took me completely by surprise when she said that doing all this 'nesting' had really made her think about what would happen if she died. Quickly checking out that she was quite well, I searched my mind as to what I could say next. Completely stumped, I simply said, 'I don't get it. Has something bad happened?' She threw back her head and laughed and said the only thing that had happened was that she'd finally grown up. As I continued to listen, Rachel explained that one evening as she and Dave were talking about whether they'd got everything ready, Dave said something about changing their will so that their child could inherit their worldly goods. This then led to their talking in more general terms about death and dying, and eventually to discussing what each of them thought they would want to happen at the end of their lives.

I asked Rachel what kind of things they'd talked about and I remember she said something like 'Just the usual sort of stuff'. When I gently pressed for a bit more detail she told me they had talked about where they wanted to be cared for at the end, and whether their spouse thought they'd be able to cope with the request. They talked about whether they wanted to be buried or cremated and whether they wanted the service in church before or after the burial/cremation. It seemed they had covered a lot of ground in their conversation and it showed that the most unlikely things can trigger discussions about death and dying.

For this couple, thinking about what would happen to their assets when they died prompted them to talk to each other about their views on how their death should be approached. Rachel and Dave were 'ordinary' people: they were not hospice patients; they were fit and well and looking forward to life, but when presented with the chance they jumped in and talked with each other about how one day they would have to face the truth that each of them would die. I hope the fact that they did this in a most informal setting – that is, in their own home, and without any external prompting – helps to illustrate how this kind of conversation can take place quite naturally and in a non-threatening way.

The final three illustrations are a little different from those already given. In the following stories we journey with the person to the end of their life. We will see how each person approached talking about death and dying, whether or not any sort of plans were made and whether or not these were carried out. We will see how the family members went about negotiating the death of their loved one and all that had to be done at that most difficult of times.

Claudia dies at home

Claudia, a long-time member of my church, was 96 when she announced to her family that she felt she did not have long left to live. She told her seven children that she felt the Lord Jesus was beginning to call her home and that she would not be sorry to go. Her husband had died some 30 years previously and she felt that now her time had come to join him. Soon afterwards, Claudia began to slow down rather rapidly and it was not many weeks before she took to her bed. The GP was called and was of the opinion that old age was taking its natural course and that it would not be surprising if Claudia died within the next few months.

At this time Claudia told her daughter that she really wanted to die at home, in her own bed with all her family round her. Those of her grown-up children, grandchildren and great-grandchildren who lived nearby agreed to work together to take care of her, with one daughter moving in to Claudia's house for the foreseeable future. The two children who lived in the USA were told about what was happening to their mother and they made plans to come and visit as soon as possible. The GP agreed to make weekly visits and to send the district nurse at least once a week. The children told the rest of the family and friends, and they settled into a routine of taking care of Claudia, who mostly stayed in bed and welcomed friends and neighbours who came to visit.

Claudia continued to say very openly that she thought she would die quite soon, so it was relatively easy for the children to talk to her about what they should do in the event of Claudia being right. She told them she'd already spoken to me, her pastor, about the funeral; she'd chosen the hymns she wanted and she expected the children to arrange a traditional Jamaican funeral. This would mean an open coffin at the funeral so people could 'pay their respects', and a burial with traditional graveside singing and filling-in of the grave. This was to be followed by a generous meal of Jamaican food offered to all of the community who wanted to come.

Four months went by and, one sunny morning, with six of her children sitting by her, Claudia passed away peacefully in her own bed. The family called the GP, who confirmed her death and issued the death certificate. As one of the children was not there and was due to fly in from the USA the next day, they asked the doctor whether they could keep Claudia at home until their brother arrived. She agreed that this would be all right but recommended that they should allow the district nurse to help them with laying out their mother's body; that they should turn off the heating in the bedroom and keep the windows closed. So this is what they did to enable their brother to say his goodbyes to his mother in her own home.

Meanwhile, they registered the death at the council office, having first phoned up to make an appointment. Two days later, they contacted the funeral director who many Jamaican families used. He took Claudia's body and the funeral was arranged. The body would be embalmed and prepared for viewing. As I had been visiting regularly right up to and including the day that Claudia died, it seemed natural to visit the family at Claudia's home to talk about the service and to pray with them. We discussed again their mother's wish for an open coffin in church and graveside singing and filling-in of the grave. I was easily able to accommodate these wishes. When a date for the funeral was fixed, the caterers were contacted and all the plans were made.

The family had been given clear instructions about what Claudia had wanted and had been able to follow them with a bit of advice from their GP regarding certain details. As Claudia made her wishes known before she went into terminal decline, there had been enough time to contact the children who lived at a distance. Communication between siblings seemed open and effective, perhaps because Claudia had led the way by being so open about facing what was happening to her. This may also have given them the confidence to enquire about whether they could keep Claudia's body at home for a few days, which is not normal practice in the UK these days. The family had been able to access spiritual support from me:

this allowed time for pastoral visits before she died and to plan the funeral according to Claudia's stated wishes. Claudia's frankness in opening the conversation about her oncoming death greatly aided the family at a time when emotions were raw and physical reserves low.

Matthew dies suddenly at home

I learnt about Matthew's story through his wife Gillian, with whom I served as a school governor at a local primary school. Matthew was only 53 when he died unexpectedly one Wednesday morning. It was a tremendous shock to everyone, not least to Gillian, who was a teaching assistant. She was at work when it happened. Matthew, who had been made redundant, had started doing woodwork and furniture restoration in his shed during the mornings.

Sometimes his great friend Sam, whom he'd known as a fellow drinker in the local pub, joined him and gave him some tips. Sam had worked in the trade before his retirement, so he knew a thing or two about working with wood. So a great deal of banter could often be heard emerging from the shed during the mornings. Perhaps that's why, when Matthew keeled over, Sam thought he was messing around. It was only when he noticed that Matthew's lips were beginning to turn blue that he realized something was very wrong. Sam gave first aid, including mouth-to-mouth resuscitation, and called an ambulance. But Matthew had died and Gillian had to be sent for and told the terrible news.

Even though Matthew had died by the time the ambulance arrived, they took him to the hospital, where he was pronounced dead on arrival. Because Matthew's death was completely unexpected and the doctors were unsure about its cause, the death had to be reported to the coroner. A&E staff explained that his body would be taken to the hospital mortuary, where a postmortem would be carried out to determine the cause of death. At this point, they asked Gillian whether she had any questions.

Desperately trying to make sense of what was going on all around her at such a pace, Gillian suddenly spurted out the words 'Organ donation'. That's all she could say. Staff then very gently probed Gillian and discovered that Matthew was on the NHS Organ Donor Register. About half an hour later, another member of staff, the organ-donation nurse, came and asked Gillian to fill in various forms that gave permission for the medics to use a number of Matthew's organs for transplantation to patients who were on the waiting list. Again the nurse asked Gillian if she had any questions. This time she said, 'Please, please can I see him afterwards?' The nurse put her arm around Gillian and assured her that would be possible, that she'd be able to spend time with Matthew and say her goodbyes.

So later that day Matthew's body went first to the organ-donations team and then to the mortuary to await the post-mortem. The next afternoon a lady from the hospital bereavement team phoned Gillian to say a death certificate had been issued and she could come and collect it. She encouraged her to do this as soon as possible so she could then register the death and make the funeral arrangements. 'Funeral arrangements?' replied Gillian. 'Yesterday we were talking about holidays in Spain. Now I just don't know what to do.' The lady from the bereavement service was very understanding and said if she could come to their office at the hospital that same day at 4 p.m., she would guide her through what needed to be done in the coming days. She said she'd explain every step of the way to her. This lady also suggested that Gillian should bring a relative or friend with her for company. 'Can I see him?' Gillian asked. The lady told her that would definitely be possible, and now that she knew Gillian wanted to do that she would make arrangements for her to see Matthew in the hospital viewing room.

So Gillian asked her sister Jackie to go with her. After they'd collected the death certificate and some helpful leaflets outlining what had to be done next, they were taken to the viewing room of the mortuary, where Gillian spent some time with Matthew. The man on duty there was very kind and, as Gillian made to leave, he said to her: 'You can come back any time. Just give us a ring. We'll look after him, until your funeral director comes to collect him.'

She didn't reply because she had no idea about funeral directors or funerals, but she knew she'd have to force herself to start thinking about it. She racked her brains to try to remember whether they'd ever talked about funerals. She had a vague memory that Matthew had once said something about woodland burial sites and how that was environmentally friendly, but she had no idea whether that would be possible. Gillian did know for certain that he would not want any kind of religious involvement and neither did she. And she said she didn't want 'one of those humanists either'; in her view they were 'just another religion'. But what *did* she want? She said she didn't really want a funeral; just a few friends to say goodbye and help her through. She then asked whether something like that would be allowed.

After talking a bit with Jackie, Gillian decided to look on the internet for some information. They found out, to their relief, that you don't have to have a funeral service if you don't want one, nor do you have to have a funeral director if you don't want one. Gillian also discovered that she could make all the arrangements herself. She wasn't sure she was up to that; she felt so drained. So they searched the internet until they found a funeral director who specialized in woodland burials, and she came to the house the next day to talk things through. This is what they agreed: there would be no funeral service, just a burial, then a reception at the pub; the funeral director would organize a grave in the local woodland burial site and would provide an environmentally friendly coffin and transport it to the burial ground on the day; she explained that Matthew's body could either stay in the hospital mortuary till the day of the funeral or be taken to her funeral director's mortuary; there would be no embalming as this was not permitted for woodland burials. Matthew's friends said they wanted to say a few words at the pub if that would be OK with Gillian. Gillian said that would be lovely.

It had been a very traumatic few days; the hardest days of her life. Gillian had had to do all her thinking from scratch because she and Matthew had not talked about their deaths in any kind of detail. At their age they didn't feel the need to do this, because, like most of us I suspect, they thought they both had years and years left before they'd die. However, in drawing on her knowledge of her husband and her thoughts and feelings, Gillian found a way of making arrangements that she felt honoured his way of living.

Larry has a heart attack at home and dies in hospital

Larry was a 75-year-old man who lived with his 70-year-old wife Ella. I got to know them both as they were regulars at the Wednesday-morning community café at my church. Larry had been told by his doctors that he had very high blood pressure and some degree of coronary heart disease. He was receiving treatment for the raised blood pressure but had been warned that he was at some risk of having a heart attack. Whether he would make a good recovery if he had a heart attack was difficult for the medics to predict.

Larry's doctor had not talked about death, nor recommended or encouraged him to make any plans for the end, but as Larry and Ella talked about his health they found themselves talking about what they should do if he had a heart attack. They discovered that they shared the view that, should this happen, every attempt to help him recover should be made. This obviously included getting Larry to hospital as soon as possible. Larry was quite clear that, even if his symptoms appeared severe and hope of recovery slim, he wanted all measures possible taken to save his life, including resuscitation. He wanted 'everything to be done'. If he died at the hospital, then so be it; but he wanted 'everything possible to be tried'.

They also talked a little about a funeral, should Larry die. They decided which funeral director they'd like to use and that, even though neither of them had a defined faith, they'd like a traditional funeral at the local church where they got married: St Bart's. Larry said he would prefer to be cremated.

One day Larry did indeed have the predicted heart attack and unfortunately it was a severe one. Ella was with him at home when it happened and immediately called 999 for an ambulance. On arrival at the house, the paramedics began resuscitation at once as Larry's heart had stopped, then transported him to A&E, where he was given further emergency treatment. He was then transferred to the coronary care unit.

After a few days, Larry was still very poorly and none of the medical interventions seemed to be having the desired effect. Ella was told that, at this stage, the outcome was very uncertain: on balance the medics felt it was unlikely Larry would recover and that he was at risk of having another heart attack which, this time, could prove fatal. Aware of Larry's wish to opt for as much medical intervention as possible, Ella said that should Larry have another heart attack she felt sure that he would again want them to attempt resuscitation. She explained this was something they had talked about and was his clear wish. Ella was able to state her case calmly, secure in the knowledge that she was doing what Larry wanted.

Sadly, Larry did have a second heart attack while in hospital. The medical team attempted resuscitation but this time it was unsuccessful and Larry died. It had been one week since he had had the first heart attack at home. Ella was naturally devastated at the loss of her husband but took great comfort in the fact that she'd known the kind of things that were important to him regarding his death, and felt she'd been able to act in accordance with his wishes.

The doctor on the ward issued a death certificate and Larry's body was taken to the hospital mortuary, where it remained for a day until Ella contacted the funeral director they had previously chosen, Joanne Jones. Joanne subsequently collected the body from the hospital and took it to the mortuary at her premises. She suggested to Ella that Larry's body should be embalmed and prepared for viewing. As Ella and Larry had not discussed this, she was content to be guided by the funeral director, whom she found she could talk to quite easily. They also talked about having the funeral at St Bart's Church and they agreed that Joanne would contact the vicar and the crematorium. She would contact Ella when she had a few possible dates pencilled in.

The day after the death, Ella made an appointment at the council offices to register the death, and her next-door neighbour June went with her. When Ella phoned up to make this appointment, the person on the phone explained what documents she'd need to bring along.

Summary

The examples presented in this chapter underline the value of considering the fact that one day we will die and the importance of talking this over with our loved ones. This would mean they then have a clearer sense of our views on death and dying, which they could work towards honouring. Feeling that you have respected your loved one's views and have succeeded in carrying them out can be a great comfort when you are grieving. Moreover, in the chaos of bereavement it is extremely helpful to have at least some clear instructions to follow. It can be argued that discussing death and dying with loved ones before we die is a win-win situation. First, it will be a great help to our relatives at a time of deep distress; and second, knowing we've lifted the weight off their shoulders of making all the decisions could bring us a measure of peace of mind.

Furthermore, for Christians both these tasks – that is, carrying out the stated wishes of the deceased and leaving guidance for surviving relatives – can be seen as a way of ministering Christian love to each other as we bear one another's burdens (Walker, 2020). All this, of course, is dependent on our taking that first basic step of accepting that death will one day come our way; and then taking the second step of finding a willingness in our hearts to talk about this.

6

The Way Ahead:
Talking About Our Own Death

In the Introduction to this book, I alluded to Leonardo da Vinci's notion of 'learning how to die' as a way of understanding the present need to actively promote open discussions and dialogues about death. I believe the need to learn how to die, to learn how to speak about death, resonates very much with this moment in Western culture and thus is the backcloth for the ideas presented in this book. Importantly, it is my firmly held view that facing the fact that one day we will die, and exploring what that might mean for us in the here and now, are positive things to do. They are things anyone can learn to do, despite the reality of self-grief and potential pain and sadness that may accompany the process. In this work of facing our mortality we may be assisted by knowledge gleaned from social theories of grief and loss, which can act a bit like a satnav in helping us understand our location within the grief process, and also help us determine which steps to take next on our onward journey. It may help us to know how others view death and to feel that we are not travelling on this journey alone but in the company of fellow passengers. As Christians we will have the framework of faith within which to place our grief and our approach to death and dying.

Christian faith speaks to the hope of a future beyond death but also to the hope of strength to get us through all the complexities, joys and sorrows of this mortal life. Christian faith is a living hope and is itself a process. Russell Herbert is of the opinion that Christian hope grows organically; the process takes time and involves moving forwards into new territory and new thoughts. This can be a painful struggle at times but is always underpinned by the surety of God's all-powerful and unending love for his people (Herbert, 2006, p. 7). Such love is most powerfully demonstrated in and attested to by the cross and resurrection of Jesus Christ. It is indeed salient to remember that Christian faith is based on a death and then a resurrection, and so not even death can separate us from God's love, as St Paul reminds us:

> For I am convinced that neither death nor life, neither angels nor demons, neither the present nor the future, nor any powers, neither height nor depth, nor anything else in all creation, will be able to separate us from the love of God that is in Christ Jesus our Lord. (Rom. 8.38–39 NIV)

The Christian's relationship with God made possible by the resurrection is the means by which we are safely held in God's heart and mind, and provides solid ground for Christian hope. It is also the key to dealing with not just the sadness we may feel when we contemplate our death but also any fear we may have about death and what lies beyond. Sam Wells maintains that it is precisely this good news about our relationship with God here and now that enables us to think about our dying with steady nerves and copious amounts of hope (Wells, 2011, pp. 7–8).

Furthermore, Christian hope in the face of death is something that the Church can offer to the world. Christians can say to the world that this is something that can be done; death can be faced. There is a prayer that is often said at the beginning of a United Reformed Church funeral service; it enjoins us to live as those who are prepared to die: 'Help us to live as those who are prepared to die, and when our days here are ended, enable us to die as those who go forth and live, so that living or dying our life may be in Jesus Christ our risen saviour' (United Reformed Church, 1999, p. 69).

The thought here is based on Romans 14.8: *whether we live or die, we belong to the Lord.* Living in the light of that thought is a witness to the world concerning our beliefs. It also provides us with a mode of living whereby our day-to-day life reflects the very real hope that faith in Jesus Christ, the risen Saviour, offers us. If we can find the faith and courage to model living as those who are prepared to die, we will find we have a powerful message to proclaim to the world. Proclaiming such a message may be viewed as prophetic.

I understand the term 'prophetic' to mean fulfilling a similar function to that of the prophets we meet within the pages of the Bible. These prophets proclaimed messages that often challenged the culture of the day by offering truths about God, humanity and the world. In this book we have seen that there are currently no agreed societal norms for talking about death, and as a topic of conversation death remains somewhat taboo. A different message spoken from a position of Christian faith that counters this viewpoint could then be prophetic. Walter Brueggemann sees the prophetic ministry of the Church as that of nurturing, nourishing and evoking a consciousness and perception that is different from the consciousness and perception of the dominant culture (2001, p. 3). In the Western world, where we are often shielded from the reality of death and where death is not routinely discussed or planned for, Christians can offer a viable alternative. Our faith gives us confidence not only to face death but also to advocate for a more open discussion of things like funerals, financial matters and what we want to happen to us at the end of our lives.

This work of encouraging conversations about death and dying also addresses and reclaims the notion of death as something natural and normative. More open and habitual discussion of the reality of death can serve to remind us that unless we die as a result of violence or a tragic accident, our death will simply mark the end of a 'normal' life: it will be neither a mistake nor a tragedy. It may be sad for those who love us, but our death will be very much part of our lives. Somehow we need to relearn this and also how to talk about it.

A preliminary step in such learning may involve simply acknowledging that resistance to routinely talking about death is subtle and pervasive. For example, even naming death seems to be a struggle for many of us. Instead of saying 'When I die', we prefer to deploy euphemisms such as 'When my number's up', 'When I kick the bucket' or '*If* something happens to me'. Although we all know logically that we are mortal and so one day will die, there can be a palpable reluctance to even naming death, never mind talking about it. But that is not to say that such hesitancy represents an insurmountable barrier. Far from it, for having acknowledged this tendency to avoid death-talk we can then start to formulate strategies to overcome it. Confident that death is a natural part of God's plan for our lives and therefore something worthy of conversation, we could make a positive decision to seek out ways to initiate a conversation about our eventual death.

Preparing to talk

So far in this book, I have purposefully shied away from providing a detailed 'How-to Guide' for talking about death and dying. Instead, I have attempted to provoke thinking about why it is important for us to reflect on how we approach death as individuals and as a society. I have attempted to get a debate going about the important ideas under consideration. This book is very much about *why* we need to think about and talk about death rather than *how* we should go about this task.

That being said, I realize that it might be helpful to have a few examples to illustrate various ways of how this task could be taken forward. Therefore, in the rest of this chapter I will give a few possible starting points for engaging in a conversation about your death and dying. I want to emphasize that the examples given below are merely starting points not blueprints for action. These illustrations and suggestions can be adapted to suit each person's individual circumstances. It may be helpful to select elements from several of these ideas and resources and tailor your approach according to your personal style, unique needs and family situation. It could be that engaging with the various examples helps you formulate a new and creative approach of your own. As with many tasks, the most important part – and sometimes the hardest – is getting started. One simple way is to read the ideas in this chapter and to reflect on what you read.

Have a conversation with yourself and with God

One way of starting the conversation is to do some thinking about all of this on your own. This has the advantage of giving you time and space to clarify your ideas. For you, it may be important to have some indication of your own thoughts and feelings about this sensitive subject, before you have to speak them out loud to your loved ones, who may respond with waves of emotion. Of course, this does not necessarily preclude remaining open to refining your ideas when you do have a discussion with others. Indeed, involving those closest to you could be a creative and loving thing to do. For example, if you subsequently find yourself having a conversation about what you might want to happen around the time of your death, this may also provide an opportunity to co-create plans around any ideas you may have about end-of-life care or your funeral.

Speaking of those closest to you, the person to whom Christians are also close (and, arguably, closest) is God, so I would highly recommend bringing God into your thinking. As Christians we believe that every aspect of our life is important to God. I firmly believe that the God who knows the very number of the hairs on our head, and who did not turn away from the cross for our sake, will not turn away when we need help thinking about the end of our earthly lives. Therefore, a frank conversation with the God who made us and loves us and whom we believe holds out a future life to us could be immensely helpful. If we feel anxious about voicing our thoughts about the end of life, we could ask God to reveal to us any particular areas of concern we may have. Talking these things over with Christian friends, or a pastor or minister, or doing some reading and praying about these specific issues, could then prove very valuable. Even re-reading Chapter 2 of this book could help to illuminate our particular issues as we remember that nothing can separate us from the love of God and that Jesus' promise of paradise to the criminal on the cross beside him holds just as true for us.

As you begin prayerfully to ponder the subject of your own death, thoughts and feelings may flow freely, and clear ideas about how to approach a conversation with your loved ones may easily come to mind. If this is not the case, though, if you feel more hesitant and unsure, then the points below may be a useful place to begin. This is not an exhaustive set of ideas; your imagination informed by the Holy Spirit may lead you exactly where *you* need to go. The suggestions are more in the nature of starter questions and signposts to thinking.

Getting started with talking about death and dying: some starter questions to consider

- Who might be the right person for you to talk with about end-of-life matters?
- Would you find it more helpful to talk with a professional or a family member? Why would this be?
- What kind of topics would you want to talk about? These might include your will, end-of-life care and funeral arrangements.
- When would be the right time to initiate such a conversation?
- When the time is right, how will you start the conversation? This might be when talking about someone who has recently died or by talking about a book or film that raises this matter.

It is worth saying a bit more about finding the right moment to open the conversation. I believe that all kinds of things that will occur in your life could act as a natural trigger to help you start talking about death. For you, the trigger might be when you move house or when you write (or rewrite) your will, or it might be when you retire, change job or start to draw your pension. It could be when you get married or when your children leave home. It may be after someone you are close to dies. I encourage you to let any or all of these significant moments in life prompt you to do something about this proposed conversation. Let one of these triggers become the moment when you make your move, when you take action, when you say: 'There's something important I'd like to talk to you about. Can we do that now?' Exercise whatever opportunity feels right for you to seize the day, to start your end-of-life conversation.

Some people find that the difficulty for them is not about finding the right time: the difficulty for them is anxiety about raising such a sensitive subject. Some may worry that they would upset their nearest and dearest if they tried to talk directly to them about mortality. Such anxieties, often internalized, can develop into a mindset of reluctance to discuss death and dying. Not wanting to upset your family and friends is very understandable, but families and friends who care for us will surely want what is best for us. If we can show the way and demonstrate that for us, talking about this is actually helpful, this will ease the way for them to be able to follow our lead and talk about whatever is important to us regarding the end of our lives. We and our families may be upset when we have the conversation or we may not; but the peace of mind we stand to gain far outweighs the momentary difficulty.

Another thing to bear in mind is that if talking face to face with our nearest and dearest is just too painful, we could record our wishes by writing them down (or through video or audio form) and then sharing that with them. I came across an interesting example of this when Tony, a member of my church, asked me to visit him at home to discuss something. When I arrived at the house, Tony explained that when he'd been round to his elderly mother's home the day before to have Sunday lunch, she'd handed him a piece of paper with the following words written on it in her old-fashioned, ultra-neat handwriting:

- No resuscitation.
- Keep me at home if you can.
- I want Susan to take the funeral.
- Put my ashes where we put Dad's.
- Love your children.

Nothing more was said between them about this, as Tony sensed that she didn't want to talk about it so he didn't ask her for further explanation. He simply took the list home. Apparently, Tony's mother, though elderly, had not become ill recently and was not in any kind of distress; she'd just decided to give him this information over lunch. I asked him how he felt about it all and Tony said he was rather surprised and at a loss as to what to do about it. When I asked whether he wanted to discuss the contents of the list with his mum he said he didn't want to question any of her decisions, because he thought she should have just what she wanted. Also, he felt he could do everything she asked without any trouble. So I suggested that the following Sunday he could mention the list in a matter-of-fact way to indicate that he was keeping it safe, and that he was very happy to do everything his mother wanted. I said I would take the funeral when the time came. So that's what Tony did. At that point his mum, apparently, just smiled and nodded and nothing more was said. It would seem that for this family, communicating in this way was perfectly adequate and appropriate. They weren't the sort of people who talked things over in great emotional depth; they were people of few words who expressed their deep feelings in down-to-earth, pragmatic ways.

Others will want to talk more about the various aspects of the end of their lives. My own family are a little more talkative and I've had several conversations with my daughter about what I want to happen at the end. I've backed this up with making a few notes for her. We've even felt comfortable discussing details about what I want to happen to my body after I've died. So there's a section in my notes that reads as follows:

- No embalming.
- You two [my daughters] can view the body if you need to, but no one else to do this.
- Try to find an environmentally friendly funeral director who will interfere as little as possible – just collect the body and deliver to the funeral.

I would argue that talking with your friends and family about your death, in whatever way is appropriate for you – either in lots of detail or in a few words, spoken or recorded – enables a level of communication and sharing that is of the 'Deep calls to deep' kind (Ps. 42.7). What is more, it is literally a once-in-a-lifetime opportunity. Indeed, including your loved ones in such a conversation means they will possess for ever the privileged status of those who shared your thoughts and feelings about a matter that was of ultimate significance to you. They will have the satisfaction of knowing that they were part of something profound in your life. Furthermore, I believe this can smooth the way into the grieving process for them and perhaps even bring some peace of mind.

Church resources for talking about end-of-life wishes

There are a number of church courses that could support you in starting your conversation. Many who have attended such courses have reported very high levels of appreciation and increased confidence in talking about death and dying (Collicutt, 2015). As yet there are not many of these death-preparation courses and schemes, but as the positive feedback from those who have engaged in such initiatives becomes more widely known, the number of them on offer looks set to grow. You could consider asking your church leadership to put on such a course for your church or access one for yourself directly.

One excellent death-preparation scheme called DeathLife is running in the Anglican diocese of Oxford (Diocese of Oxford, 2020). This scheme aims to equip churches and individuals to explore issues around death with greater confidence. Embedded in this is the notion that death-talk is for everyone at every stage of life and not exclusively for people who are frail, elderly or terminally ill. Interestingly, it sees the act of preparing for death while still in the midst of life as a natural part of discipleship. Hence, DeathLife encourages participants to take time to reflect theologically on their mortality. The idea here is that if death is a natural part of our life, then it can be regarded as a natural part of our walk with God. The DeathLife section of the diocese's website quotes people who found that participating in the course reinforced a sense of human solidarity and that it was helpful to be reminded that we are all on the same journey. Other benefits noted by participants included that the course helped affirm their identity as individuals; it helped them to go deeper into their Christian faith, including any fear of dying, and it provided a safe place to discuss matters they had been putting off, or been prevented from, discussing as a result of barriers erected by distressed family members.

DeathLife offers a range of resources. There is the opportunity for attending a one-off, two-hour workshop for up to 15 adults that encourages people to get talking about death through the use of art, music, poetry and Scripture. Then there is a six-week course whereby up to 12 people meet for a two-hour session. The sessions are entitled Be Prepared; The Story of My Life; Planning My Funeral; The Last Days; Departing in Peace; and What Comes Next. The website also helpfully provides a range of ready-made material, such as Bible studies and sermon starters on topics that include letting go and having hope.

Another useful resource that may appeal to you is Grave Talk, from the Church of England, which offers a café space where people can talk about end-of-life matters. Grave Talk's viewpoint is that although it may not be easy to talk about death, dying and funerals, if we neglect these subjects we can be unprepared for the most significant events we will ever have to face – that is, our own death and the deaths of those close to us (Millar, 2015).

In this scheme a church puts on a Grave Talk event in a church hall, community centre or neighbourhood café. People attending such an event are welcomed by someone from the church and then invited to sit at tables with three or four others with whom they will talk about things relating to the end of life. Light refreshments are offered throughout the event, which lasts about an hour. The conversation is helped along by Grave Talk starter cards that have earlier been placed on the table. Each group picks a question from the cards on offer and people are invited to talk about the subject and to listen to one another. The 52 cards each have a thought-provoking and open-ended question covering different key areas, including: Life; Death; Society; Funerals; and Grief. The questions vary greatly, and some are of a rather general nature – such as 'How has our culture shaped our thinking about death?' Others are more personal – such as 'What music would you like to have played or sung at your funeral?'

Originally piloted in the diocese of Lichfield in 2014, Grave Talk has grown in popularity across the Anglican Church but is of course available for use in churches of all denominations. There has also been some uptake in the secular world, where it has been used in settings such as hospices, prisons and social care situations. Indeed, a secular agency that provides training for care workers has used it as part of their assessment pro-gramme for potential workers and apprentices (Millar, 2016). Such crossover from the world of the Church to the secular world shows that those outside of Christianity can still find worth in our way of approaching end-of-life issues. More-over, it demonstrates that speaking about end-of-life matters underlines our common humanity and our common mortality. Discussion around the end of life, then, has the potential to make connections with different groups in society and to provide an opportunity for dialogue between them.

Secular resources for talking about the end of life

In a similar vein, you may find it helpful to access information and materials from secular sources. In Chapter 4, I mentioned that a number of resources and schemes have arisen in recent years that reflect society's gradually increasing interest in talking about end-of-life matters. The Death Café movement is one example of such a scheme. Death Café meetings are open to everyone and are held at various venues up and down the country, including homes, coffee shops, art galleries and community halls. A conversation about death is facilitated by an organizer. The stated objective of the Death Café movement is 'to increase awareness of death with a view to helping people make the most of their [finite] lives' (Death Café, 2022). The group discussion about death purposely has no agenda, objectives or themes. It is made clear that this is a discussion group rather than a grief-support or counselling session. If discussing end-of-life matters with no Christian input and with a group of people who would not attend a church gathering is important to you, going to a Death Café meeting may have appeal.

Another valuable source of information from the secular world is the Dying Matters Campaign. Dying Matters was started in 2009 as a coalition of individuals and organizational members across England and Wales, aiming to help people talk more openly about dying, death and bereavement, and to make plans for the end of life. Information about Dying Matters can be accessed through the Hospice UK website (https://www.hospiceuk.org/our-campaigns/dying-matters). Those who support the campaign include organizations from across the NHS, voluntary and independent health and care sectors (including hospices, care homes and charities supporting old people, children and bereavement).

In addition to providing materials that could assist with end-of-life conversations, an integral part of the mission of Dying Matters is to work for a fundamental change in society in which dying, death and bereavement will be seen and accepted as natural parts of everybody's life cycle. One major annual event that attempts to improve this situation is the Dying Matters Awareness Week, which runs every May. Through this initiative the Dying Matters campaign promotes a wide programme of events about death, dying and bereavement across the country. For example, there has been a Death Festival at London's South Bank that featured debates, readings, puppet shows and an international coffin exhibition. Meanwhile, in Birmingham, a group called You Only Die Once (YODO) took a 'Before I Die Wall' into libraries, shops and city streets on which people of all ages could write their life ambitions, hopes and dreams. This group ended their week with a Death Disco at which people could add songs that have been meaningful in their lives to the disco's playlist.

Some commentators think that the Dying Matters campaign is contributing to death becoming a more prominent subject in the national conversation (Elmhirst, 2015). Although a lot of its information seems to be particularly relevant to those who will soon be approaching the end of their life, the campaign's aim is to be accessible to everyone. The website sections on 'How to Open Up Difficult Conversations' and 'How to Listen Well' are particularly applicable to anyone at any stage of life who wishes to discuss end-of-life matters.

Medical matters, wills, funerals and end-of-life conversations

In the Introduction, I emphasized that this book is not primarily concerned with medical matters pertaining to the end of life, nor is it concerned with writing a will or planning a funeral. However, I recognize that such concerns might form part of a conversation about end-of-life considerations, so I now wish to say a brief word about recent resources that can help address them.

Some people will want to consider what kinds of medical interventions and treatments they feel they will want to have (or not have) as they approach the end of their lives. Two documents in particular that are readily available to the public can help people to record such choices. These are:

- Advance Decisions to Refuse Treatment;
- Lasting Power of Attorney for Health and Care Decisions.

An Advance Decision to Refuse Treatment (ADRT), formerly known as a Living Will or Advance Directive, is where you make a decision to refuse a specific type of medical intervention at some point in the future. This decision must be signed by you and witnessed by someone else. Your ADRT would only come into play if you lost the ability to make your own decision at the time the treatment became relevant (NHS, 2020).

A Lasting Power of Attorney (LPA) for Health and Care Decisions gives another person the legal right to make decisions about your personal welfare should you lose the ability to make specific health and welfare decisions for yourself (Office of the Public Guardian, 2022). Such health and care decisions might include giving or refusing consent to healthcare; staying in your own home and getting help and support from social services; moving into residential care; finding a good care home; and day-to-day matters such as your diet, clothing or daily routine. It is important to understand that your appointed attorney can only make decisions when you don't have mental capacity.

With regard to financial matters, some people may want to have something in writing to support their wishes if they reach a stage when they can no longer make decisions for themselves. If this is a concern for you, it is possible to register a Lasting Power of Attorney for Financial Decisions (Office of the Public Guardian, 2022), by which you can nominate someone to act for you if you can no longer understand financial matters or make decisions about them. Such decisions might include opening, closing and using bank accounts; claiming, receiving and using benefits, pensions and allowances; paying household and care bills; making investments (or drawing on them); and buying or selling your home.

It is important to bear in mind that you must have mental capacity to register any kind of LPA. 'Mental capacity' means having the ability to make a specific decision at the time it needs to be made. So a person with mental capacity would have at least a general understanding of the decision they need to make; why they need to make it; any information relevant to the decision; and what is likely to happen when they make it. They should be able to communicate their decision through speech, signs and gestures, or in other ways (Mental Capacity Act, 2005).

Some people may find that talking about the end of their life motivates them to write or update their will. There is a wealth of information about will-writing that is easily available. A quick Google search will direct you to many and varied charities that provide advice about will-writing. Additionally, the UK government's website (gov.uk) is another place to make a start with this (UK Government, 2021).

Funerals are often mentioned when people start talking about end-of-life matters. As noted in Chapter 3, Christians sometimes talk to their ministers about the kind of funeral they think they'd like. In my experience this usually means they tell the minister what particular hymns and Bible readings they would like to be included at the church service. If this is something that you would find helpful, I would encourage you to go ahead and do it. However, you may want to make plans about other aspects of your funeral, such as who is to attend, whether you want there to be refreshments afterwards or whether you want to make use of the services of a funeral director and so on. Such options could be explored by contacting funeral directors themselves or by accessing their websites. Various church denominations also produce resources to help you consider your funeral. For example, the Church of England website (2022) has some helpful and accessible information about funeral planning, as does the Methodist Church website (2020).

One way of drawing together all your thinking about your own eventual death and what you want to happen to you at the end of your life is to write your thoughts down in an end-of-life plan. Such a document could be used as a catalyst to starting an end-of-life conversation with your friends and family. For example, you could explain that you want to share your end-of-life plan with someone and you would like to know their thoughts on what you've put in it. Or you could ask someone to help you complete your end-of-life plan, or use the plan as an exercise in trying out your own thoughts before you open a conversation in a different way. I have generated such a plan, which is published elsewhere (Walker, 2020, pp. 23–6), and similar material is available from a variety of sources. For example, the Dying Matters website (now hospiceuk.org) has very informative and useful information on planning ahead, as does the NHS website (2021).

Summary

In this chapter I have encouraged some practical thinking around learning how to die. I hope I have helped you to start or refine considering *how* to talk to your friends and family about your death. From a starting point of Christian hope in the resurrection and Christian faith that emboldens us to undertake this sensitive task, we have considered various strategies. These have included: talking to God; reflecting on our thoughts privately; and accessing helpful resources from both the Church and the secular world. Additionally, some attention has been given to concerns around 'putting our house in order' with issues of wills, financial matters, funerals and our specific end-of-life wishes.

Specifically, I hope this has at the very least provoked some concrete and direct thinking about our inevitable deaths. As Christians, we do this of course in the sure and certain knowledge that as we face the mystery of death, we also face a future eternal life, won for us by Jesus at Calvary. It is my great hope that this will enable us to confront any fears we may have and confidently engage with the task of thinking and talking about the end of our lives.

Conclusion

A Few Last Words

In this book I've been trying to make a persuasive argument in favour of getting people to think and talk about the unavoidable fact of death. I fervently hope that this has persuaded readers that contemplating the end of life long before the end is in sight is a worthwhile task, and that they will now feel better equipped to make a start on this important work. I also hope that readers who are members of the clergy, or who are healthcare chaplains or have some kind of pastoral care role, will now feel better equipped to encourage those in their care to engage in thinking and talking about their future death.

I have alluded to Leonardo da Vinci's phrase 'learning how to die' as a vivid way of encapsulating the nature of the task, and I've argued that doing this is within everyone's grasp. However, as I have already said, I recognize that this may not be easy for some, and I have enormous sympathy for those who have a very real need to deny that death is coming their way. It seems that this attitude contains within it a good measure of fear of the unknown. I sympathize. Fear of the unknown can be very real and can paralyse people into avoidance, denial and inaction. It's a sort of protective mechanism that can seduce someone into believing that if something is too frightening to contemplate, then the best thing they can do is not contemplate it. If they don't think about it, it might never happen. But with death, we know that's not true. We will all die. I believe, however, that although it might be a difficult subject to face, confronting the facts within a framework of Christian hope can help dispel fear. Just as when a child is frightened that there might be monsters under their bed, and shining a torch under the bed can demonstrate that there's nothing there that can hurt them, a little courage and knowledge can shine the light on what can seem so frightening to many people.

It may help to remember that, for a Christian, death is not a medical battle to be fought and ultimately lost. It is not a 'negative patient outcome'. Nor is it only about mourning the loss of relationships, presence and activity in the world. Facing the prospect of one's own death could also be an opportunity to work out what faith in Jesus Christ is all about. Death – why it happens and where God is in this process – is a basic concern of religious faith. It is also a profound question to consider, and coming to terms with this may involve swimming in deeper waters than we have dared to venture into before.

It may help to read about or talk with those who have known the fear of death and have come to some sort of accommodation with it under God. Many people of faith have faced the issue of death and have had their fear turned into something more positive. I count myself in their number, and so I offer a personal perspective on facing death in the light of my Christian faith. I have always found the words of Jesus on the cross to the man being crucified next to him a tremendous comfort and inspiration: 'Truly I tell you, today you will be with me in paradise' (Luke 23.43).

For me, these are words to cling to. They are a succinct expression of my faith that beyond death I know where I'm going and, more importantly, I know *who* I'm going to. This helps me not to be afraid. I believe that after a merciful judgement I will be re-created to live with God in the next life. This is the sure and certain hope of resurrection to eternal life demonstrated by Jesus' own rising from the dead. That is not to say, though, that I don't experience 'wobbles' from time to time. Indeed, there are moments and occasional days when I feel anxious or even fearful at the prospect of death. For example, I have often struggled with the passage in Philippians 1.20–23 where Paul seems to be saying that dying will be better than living, because when we die we get to be with Jesus. I *do* want to be with Jesus, I *do* want to live where there will be no more pain, tears or death (Rev. 21.4), but the thought of being separated from those I love most in this world holds me back. Like anyone else I know the ache of grief and I have prayed fervently for my loved ones to live, even if it's just for one more day. My way of coming to terms with the notion of death and the conflicting emotions that it engenders is simply to live within the apparent contradiction.

This entails trying to live every day in the confidence of a post-death resurrection, but I don't think I've failed on those days when life's many insistent voices seem to have a stronger sway over me. On days when clinging to life seems to be supremely important and death seems to be something that should be fervently resisted, I simply trust that the God who loves me will understand this and will minister to me.

Accepting the contradiction and knowing that sometimes this has to be worked with has not only turned fear into something more positive, it has also helped to build resilience. An example from my personal life may help illustrate how this can work out in practice. My older daughter, Jessica, lives with a life-limiting condition that has seriously threatened her life on several occasions. When, aged seven, she was in real danger of death, I struggled to find an authentic way to pray. I felt extremely conflicted and at the mercy of my emotions. A relative of mine who had lost two children of her own shared the following technique with me, which I found extremely helpful. I visualized my daughter going through the school gates, holding hands with Jesus and being happily led away from me. I knew that whether she lived or died she was safe and being looked after by Jesus, who loved her as much as I did. I share this here in the hope that others will find this a useful and non-frightening way of thinking about dying. This has been part of how I have been 'learning how to die'. I suspect my learning will be ongoing, and I sincerely hope that this book has helped you to progress your own learning.

In summary, then, while it may be natural to react strongly to the thought of death and dying, I encourage readers to make thinking and talking about death part of their thinking, part of their theology. Our best guide must surely be to follow the advice given in the Bible that we should grieve, but we should also have hope. As Keller (2020) asserts, this will help us to let go of any death-denying tendencies and instead embrace the peace that God offers. We need to remember that as Christians we believe God loves us here and now, and that he will know and love us in the next life too. In that, there is nothing to fear.

Further Resources

This section comprises a short list of resources (organized alphabetically) for those who wish to do some more detailed thinking around how to talk with people about death and how to approach some of the sensitive issues this may raise. The resources listed below include tools that could help initiate conversations with people about death and dying; some are concerned with practical matters such as writing a will, whereas others are organizations that offer support to people who may find entering into discussions about death difficult or upsetting.

Readers who would like to read more broadly about death, and perhaps to engage with the more academic and secular literature on this topic, will find a short bibliography of books on the theology of death. There is also a short bibliography of books on the pastoral care of the dying.

Organizations

Age UK

Provides advice on funerals and end-of-life conversations and planning end-of-life care.
https://www.ageuk.org.uk

Association of Hospice and Palliative Care Chaplains (AHPCC)

Local hospice chaplains can be great people to contact for help with talking about end-of-life matters. They are often willing to meet with local groups of clergy, pastoral carers and church-goers in order to further awareness of their own work and to foster good practice among churches. The AHPCC website provides details of regional groups of chaplains in addition to many helpful resources.
https://www.ahpcc.co.uk

Care for the Family

This is a Christian organization that provides support in various areas of family life including bereavement. It offers courses, resources and a phoneline.
https://www.careforthefamily.org.uk

Citizens Advice

Information about writing a will.
https://www.citizensadvice.org.uk

Compassion in Dying

Has information on planning ahead.
https://www.compassionindying.org.uk

Death Café movement

This is a non-profit secular organization that facilitates social events where people talk about death. It is not a grief-support or counselling group but a directed discussion. Attendance is open to all. Its website states that its objective is to increase awareness of death with a view to helping people make the most of their lives.
https://deathcafe.com

Directgov

Provides information about making a will.
https://www.direct.gov.uk

End of Life Doula UK

End of life Doulas are a relatively new and growing phenomenon in the UK. The End of Life Doula UK website states that Doulas offer non-medical, non-religious support to people with a terminal diagnosis. Doulas work in people's homes and sometimes in hospices, hospitals and care homes, alongside other healthcare and social care professionals. This organization usually makes a charge for its work.
https://eol-doula.uk

Dying Matters

This is a campaign across England and Wales that aims to help people talk more openly about dying, death and bereavement and to make plans for the end of life. Originating as a coalition of individuals and organizations in 2009, and now operating under the auspices of Hospice UK, Dying Matters provides many useful resources, including leaflets, films and reports that can help people have conversations and make plans for the future. Campaign information and resources can be accessed through the Hospice UK website.
https://www.hospiceuk.org/our-campaigns/dying-matters

Good Grief Festival

This is an annual virtual festival that explores the many faces of grief. The programme usually includes up to 70 speakers and 50 free online events that aim to help people in the UK and elsewhere who are grieving.
https://goodgrieffest.com

Hospices

Many larger hospices will have an education department offering courses that may be open to local clergy and pastoral carers. Most hospices have libraries containing helpful resources on palliative care and they may be willing to allow you access.

Hospice UK

This is a national charity that supports the work of over 200 hospices across the UK. It supports research and innovation through its annual research conference, grants and publications. The website provides a useful window into the world of hospice care.
https://www.hospiceuk.org

Marie Curie

In addition to the provision of hospice care, Marie Curie carries out research in palliative and end-of-life care, and its website has useful resources on preparing for the end of life.
https://www.mariecurie.org.uk

MHA (Methodist Homes Association)

The chaplaincy section of the website contains useful resources on approaches to end-of-life care, death and dying. It calls its approach 'The Final Lap'.
https://www.mha.org.uk/files/8316/1968/3905/MH10859_EndOfLife_Care_Strategy210x297mm_final.pdf
(accessed 15.07.2022)

National Association of Funeral Directors

https://www.nafd.org.uk

Natural Death Centre

This is a social, entrepreneurial, educational charity that gives free impartial advice on all aspects of dying, bereavement and consumer rights. There are lots of resources available via its website. Its seminal book, *The Natural Death Handbook* (by Stephanie Wienrich, 2003, New York: Vintage), is now in its fifth edition.

https://www.naturaldeath.org.uk

NHS Blood and Transplant

Gives details about organ donation.

https://www.organdonation.nhs.uk

NHS Choices

This website has information on Advance Care Planning (ACP).

https://www.nhs.uk

Office of the Public Guardian

Information regarding Lasting Powers of Attorney (LPAs).

https://www.publicguardian.gov.uk

ReSPECT documentation

This is a relatively new document from the NHS in which a summary of personal wishes for a person's clinical care in a future emergency can be recorded. *ReSPECT* stands for Recommended Summary Plan for Emergency Care and Treatment. It could be used as a helpful way into initiating a more general conversation around death and dying.

https://www.resus.org.uk/respect

Books, articles, programmes and courses

Ask NT Wright Anything

See Justin Brierley's programme on Premier Radio, *Ask NT Wright Anything*, as Tom Wright responds to the question 'My father died: where is he now?'
https://www.youtube.com/watch?v=y_T1NQ2qwE8
(accessed 04.04.2022)

Acorn Christian Healing Foundation: Listening Academy

Good listening skills are essential when talking with people about the sensitive topic of death. There are several ways to update one's skills – for example, there are plenty of books on the market on this topic. There are also courses in listening skills. For example, Acorn Christian Healing Foundation's Listening Academy aims to provide training to equip people to support others by practising excellent listening. Some church denominations run courses on listening for those involved in pastoral care.
https://acornchristian.org

Grave Talk

The Church of England website contains useful information about how to host a Grave Talk event, which is a café space where people are encouraged to talk about what they call 'life's big issues', including death, dying and bereavement.
https://www.churchofengland.org/life-events/funerals/after-funeral/what-gravetalk

Grove Booklet (P163), Talking About End-of-Life Wishes

This is a booklet I recently wrote and includes a sample end-of-life care plan and other useful tips, such as how to ensure your next of kin knows the whereabouts of your important documents and what to expect from a funeral director. See Susan Walker, 2020, *Talking About End-of-Life Wishes: Not If, But When*, Cambridge: Grove.

Books on the theology of death

Badham, P., 2013, *Making Sense of Death and Immortality*, London: SPCK.

Davies, D. J., 2007, *The Theology of Death*, Edinburgh: T&T Clark.

Guthrie, N. (ed.), 2011, *O Love That Wilt Not Let Me Go*, Wheaton, IL: Crossway.

Herbert, R. G., 2006, *Living Hope: A Practical Theology of Hope for the Dying*, London: Epworth Press.

Jones, D. A., 2007, *Approaching the End: A Theological Exploration of Death and Dying*, Oxford: Oxford University Press.

Jupp, P., 2008, *Death Our Future: Christian Theology and Funeral Practice*, London: Epworth Press.

Keller, T., 2020, *On Death*, London: Hodder & Stoughton.

Marshall, P., 2017, *Invisible Worlds: Death, Religion and the Supernatural*, London: SPCK.

Mascall, E., 1961, *Grace and Glory*, London: Faith Press.

Moll, R., 2010, *The Art of Dying: Living Fully Into the Life to Come*, Downers Grove, IL: InterVarsity Press.

Nichols, T., 2010, *Death and Afterlife: A Theological Introduction*, Grand Rapids, MI: Brazos Press.

Pittenger, N., 2012, *After Death: Life in God*, London: SCM Press.

Proctor, J., 2012, *Over the Horizon*, 2nd edn, Poole: GEAR Publications.

Walker Bynum, C., 1996, *The Resurrection of the Body in Western Christianity, 200–1336*, New York: Columbia University Press.

Williamson, P. R., 2017, *Death and the Afterlife*, Leicester: IVP.

Wright, Tom, 2009, *Surprised by Hope: Rethinking Heaven, the Resurrection and the Mission of the Church*, London: SPCK.

Books on the pastoral care of the dying

Ainsworth-Smith, I. and P. Speck, 1999, *Letting Go: Caring for the Dying and Bereaved*, London: SPCK.

Albom, M., 1997, *Tuesdays With Morrie: An Old Man, a Young Man and Life's Greatest Lessons*, New York: Doubleday.

Callanan, M. and P. Kelly, 1992, *Final Gifts: Understanding the Special Awareness, Needs and Communications of the Dying*, London: Hodder & Stoughton.

Cassidy, S., 1998, *Sharing the Darkness: The Spirituality of Caring*, London: Darton, Longman & Todd.

Cobb, M., 2001, *The Dying Soul: Spiritual Care at the End of Life*, Oxford: Oxford University Press.

Evans, S. and A. Davison, 2014, *Care for the Dying: A Practical and Pastoral Guide*, Norwich: Canterbury Press.

Lewis, C. S., 1961, *A Grief Observed*, London: Faber & Faber.

Murray, D., 2002, *Faith in Hospices: Spiritual Care and the End of Life*, London: SPCK.

Neuberger, J., 2004, *Caring for Dying People of Different Faiths*, Abingdon: Radcliffe Medical Press.

Saunders, C., 2005, *Watch with Me: Inspiration for a Life in Hospice Care*, Lancaster: International Observatory on End of Life Care (IOELC).

Tan, S. (ed.), 2013, *Soul Pain: Priests Reflect on Personal Experiences of Serious and Terminal Illness*, Norwich: Canterbury Press.

Universities

For readers who would like to engage with the academic secular work around death and dying, certain universities could prove helpful. Some are developing a particular interest in end-of-life matters and can signpost you to recent publications and current research in this area. For example, the University of Durham has a Centre for Death and Life Studies (https://www.durham.ac.uk/research/institutes-and-centres/death-life-studies). This centre aims to foster and conduct research into life values, beliefs and practices that relate to living and dying. Similarly, the University of Bath's Centre for Death & Society (https://www.bath.ac.uk/research-centres/centre-for-death-society) specializes in interdisciplinary aspects of death, dying and bereavement.

Bibliography

Aulen, G., 1931, *Christus Victor*, London: SPCK.

Barth, K., 1966, *Church Dogmatics in Outline*, London: SCM Press.

Barth, K., 2009, *Church Dogmatics*, 4 vols, New York: T&T Clark.

Bingham J., 2014, 'Queen's birthday card team expands to cope with surge of 100-year-olds', *The Telegraph*, 25 September, https://www.telegraph.co.uk/news/health/elder/11121184/Queens-birthday-card-team-expands-to-cope-with-surge-of-100-year-olds.html (accessed 6.07.2022).

Brueggemann, W., 2001, *The Prophetic Imagination*, 2nd edn, Minneapolis, MN: Fortress Press.

Care Act 2014 c. 23, available at: https://www.legislation.gov.uk/ukpga/2014/23/contents/enacted (accessed 15.07.2022).

Casalis, C., 2022, 'Prepaid funeral plans', *Money Saving Expert*, 17 June, https://www.moneysavingexpert.com/family/prepaid-funeral-plans/ (accessed 06.07.2022).

Church of England, 2002, *Common Worship: Daily Prayer*, London: Church House Publishing.

Church of England website, 2022, https://www.churchofengland.org/life-events/funerals/funeral-service-step-step#with-you-at-every-step (accessed 18.08.22).

Cobb, M., 2005, *The Hospital Chaplain's Handbook*, Norwich: Canterbury Press.

Collicutt, J., 2015, 'Living in the end times: a short course addressing end of life issues for older people in an English parish church setting', *Working with Older People*, 19 (3), pp. 140–9, https://doi.org/10.1108/WWOP-11-2014-0034.

Collicutt, J., 2019, 'Lessons on the art of dying well', *Church Times*, 18 October, https://www.churchtimes.co.uk/articles/2019/18-october/features/features/lessons-on-the-art-of-dying-well (accessed 10.04.2020).

ComRes, 2016, *Dying Matters Coalition – Public Opinion on Death and Dying*, https://comresglobal.com/wp-content/uploads/2016/05/NCPC_Public-polling-2016_Data-tables.pdf (accessed 11.07.2022).

Death Café, 2022, 'What is Death Café?', https://deathcafe.com/what/ (accessed 13.10.22).

Desharnais, S. and colleagues, 2007, 'Lack of concordance between physician and patient: reports on end-of-life care discussions', *Journal of Palliative Medicine*, 10 (3), pp. 728–40.

Diabetes UK, 'Free Wills', *Diabetes UK*, https://www.diabetes.org.uk/get_involved/ways-to-donate/leaving-a-legacy/free-wills-month (accessed 12.10.2020).

Diocese of Oxford, DeathLife, 2020, https://www.oxford.anglican.org/mission/deathlife/.

Doughty, K., 2014, *Smoke Gets In Your Eyes*, London: W. W. Norton.

Elmhirst, S., 2015, 'Take me to the Death Café', *Prospect Magazine*, 22 January, https://www.prospectmagazine.co.uk/magazine/take-me-to-the-death-cafe (accessed 04.03.2020).

Evans, S. and Davison, A., 2014, *Care for the Dying*, Norwich: Canterbury Press.

Field, A., Finucane, A. and Oxenham, D., 2013, 'Discussing preferred place of death with patients: staff experiences in a UK specialist palliative care setting', *International Journal of Palliative Nursing*, 19 (11), pp. 558–65.

Ford, H., 2020, 'What should a dying patient and family members do?', https://www.henryford.com/-/media/files/henry-ford/patients-visitors/what-should-a-dying-patient-and-family-members-do-islam.pdf?la=en&hash=E04311D89BF2257047303F (accessed 27.07.2020).

Gawande, A., 2015, *Being Mortal: Illness, Medicine and What Matters in the End*, London: Wellcome Trust.

Gold Standards Framework, 2016, 'The Gold Standards Framework', https://www.goldstandardsframework.org.uk (accessed 02.02.2019).

Gomes, B., Calanzani, N. and Higginson I. J., 2012, 'Reversal of the British trends in place of death: time series analysis 2004–2010', *Palliative Medicine*, 26 (2), pp. 102–7, https://doi.org/10.1177/0269216311432329.

Gorer, G., 1965, *Death, Grief and Mourning in Contemporary Britain*, London: Cresset.

Grimaldo, D. A. and colleagues, 2001, 'A randomized, controlled trial of advanced care planning discussions during preoperative evaluations', *Anesthesiology*, 95 (1), pp. 43–50.

Gutheil, I. A. and Heyman, J. C., 2005, 'Communication between older people and their health care agents: results of an intervention', *Health Social Work*, 3 (2), pp. 107–16.

Heine, S. J. and colleagues, 2006, 'The meaning maintenance model: on the coherence of social motivations', *Personality and Social Psychology Review*, 10 (2), pp. 88–110.

Herbert, R. G., 2006, *Living Hope: A Practical Theology of Hope for the Dying*, London: Epworth Press.

Hospice UK, 2020, 'Information and support', *Hospice UK*, https://www.hospiceuk.org/information-and-support (accessed 15.07.2022).

Hospice UK, 2021, 'Planning ahead', *Hospice UK*, https://www.hospiceuk.org/information-and-support/your-guide-hospice-and-end-life-care/planning-ahead (accessed 15.07.2022).

Irvine, W. B., 2009, *A Guide to the Good Life: The Ancient Art of Stoic Joy*, Oxford: Oxford University Press.

John, J., 2001, *The Meaning in the Miracles*, Norwich: Canterbury Press.

Jones, L. and colleagues, 2011, 'Advance care planning in advanced cancer: can it be achieved? An exploratory randomized patient preference trial of a care planning discussion', *Palliative and Supportive Care*, 9 (1), pp. 3–13.

Kearney, M., 1990, 'Spiritual pain', *The Way*, 30 (1), pp. 47–54.

Keller, T., 2020, *On Death*, London: Hodder & Stoughton.

Kübler-Ross, E., 1969, *On Death and Dying*, New York: Macmillan.

Lewis, C. S., 1952, *Mere Christianity*, London: Macmillan.

Lloyd, M., 2020, *Café Theology: Exploring Love, the Universe and Everything*, London: Hodder & Stoughton.

Macmillan Cancer Support, 'Macmillan Free Will Service', *Macmillan Cancer Support*, https://www.macmillan.org.uk/donate/gifts-in-wills/free-will-service.html (accessed 12.10.2020).

Marie Curie, 2011, 'Caring Together Programme', *Marie Curie*, https://www.mariecurie.org.uk/professionals/commissioning-our-services/partnerships-innovations/current/caring-together (accessed 6.07.2022).

Marshall, A., 2017a, *My Mourning Year: A Memoir of Bereavement, Discovery and Hope*, Brentford: Red Door Publishing.

Marshall, A., 2017b, 'Five reasons I decided to write about myself', 30 January, https://andrewgmarshall.com/five-reasons-i-decided-write-about-myself/ (accessed 20.07.2022).

Mental Capacity Act 2005 c. 9, available at: https://www.legislation.gov.uk/ukpga/2005/9/notes/contents (accessed 15.07.2022).

Methodist Church website, 2020, 'Funerals', *The Methodist Church*, https://www.methodist.org.uk/our-faith/life-and-faith/life-events/funerals/ (accessed 02.02.2016).

Millar, S., 2015, *Grave Talk Facilitator's Guide*, London: Church House Publishing.

Millar, S., 2016, 'Let's all talk about death', *Church Times*, https://www.churchtimes.co.uk/articles/2016/6-may/comment/opinion/lets-all-talk-about-death (accessed 15.07.2022).

Moll, R., 2010, *The Art of Dying: Living Fully Into the Life to Come*, Downers Grove, IL: InterVarsity Press.

Money Helper, 'Death and Bereavement', *Money Helper*, https://www. moneyhelper.org.uk/en/family-and-care/death-and-bereavement? source=mas (accessed 15.07.2022).

Money Saving Expert, 2020, https://www.moneysavingexpert.com/ family/prepaid-funeral-plans/ (accessed 28.07.2020).

Moss, B., 2005, *Religion and Spirituality*, Lyme Regis: Russell House Publishing.

Munday D., Petrova, M. and Dale, J., 2009, 'Exploring preferences for place of death with terminally ill patients', *British Medical Journal*, 339:b2391.

NHS, 2020, 'Advance Decision (living will)', *NHS*, https://www.nhs. uk/conditions/end-of-life-care/advance-decision-to-refuse-treatment (accessed 12.10.2020).

NHS, 2021, 'End of Life Care', *NHS*, https://www.nhs.uk/Planners/ end-of-life-care/Pages/planning-ahead.aspx/ (accessed 15.07.2022).

National Institute for Clinical Excellence (NICE), 2004, *Guidance on Cancer Services: Improving Supportive and Palliative Care for Adults*, London: NICE.

Office of the Public Guardian, 2022, 'Lasting Power of Attorney forms', *gov.uk*, https://www.gov.uk/government/publications/make-a-lasting-power-of-attorney (accessed 15.07.2022).

Ott, P. W., 1989, 'John Wesley on mind and body: towards an understanding of health as wholeness', *Methodist History*, 27 (2), pp. 61–73.

Parker, R., Fraser, D. and Rivers, D., 2003, *In Search of Wholeness*, Nottingham: St John's Extension Studies.

Parliamentary and Health Service Ombudsman, 2015, 'Dying Without Dignity', https://www.ombudsman.org.uk/reports-and-consultations/ reports/health/dying-without-dignity (accessed 15.02.2016).

Polkinghorne, J., 2002, *The God of Hope and the End of the World*, London: SPCK.

Proctor, J., 2012, *Over the Horizon*, 2nd edn, Poole: GEAR Publications.

Read, S. and Elliott, D., 2007, 'Exploring a continuum of support for bereaved people with intellectual disabilities: A strategic approach', *Journal of Intellectual Disabilities*, 11 (2), pp. 167–81. DOI:10.1177/ 1744629507076930.

Russell, B., 1946, *A History of Western Philosophy*, London: Routledge.

Saunders, C., 1978, *The Management of Terminal Disease*, London: Edward Arnold.

Saunders, C., 2003, *Watch with Me: Inspiration for a Life in Hospice Care*, Lancaster: International Observatory on End of Life Care (IOELC).

Shinners, J., 1997, 'The Art of Dying Well', in John Shinners (ed.), *Medieval Popular Religion, 1000–1500, a Reader*, London: Broadview Press, pp. 525–35.

Stroebe, M. and Schut, H., 1999, 'The dual process model of coping with bereavement: rationale and description', *Death Studies*, 23 (3), pp. 197–204.

The, A. M. and colleagues, 2000, 'Collusion in doctor-patient communication about imminent death: an ethnographic study', *British Medical Journal*, 321, pp. 1376–81.

Thompson-Hill, J. and colleagues, 2009, 'The supportive care plan: a tool to improve communication in end-of-life care', *International Journal of Palliative Nursing*, 15 (5), pp. 250–5.

Townshend, T., 2018, 'What death can teach us about preaching', *Liturgy*, 33 (1), pp. 49–55.

UK Government, 2021, 'Making a will', *gov.uk*, https://www.gov.uk/make-will (accessed 29.09.2021).

United Reformed Church, 1999, *The Service Book*, London: United Reformed Church.

Walker, S. and Flanagan, P., 2009, 'Do you want to make the decision about where you want to die or do you want someone else to make it?', in *Making Life Before Death Matter*, Help the Hospices Conference, Harrogate, 24–26 November, London: Help the Hospices.

Walker, S., 2016, *Finding a Voice at the End of Life: Exploring Preferred Place of Death in a Hospice Context*, Keele: Keele University.

Walker, S., 2020, *Talking About End-of-life Wishes: Not If, But When*, Cambridge: Grove.

Walter, T., 1991, 'Modern death: taboo or not taboo?', *Sociology*, 25 (2), pp. 293–310.

Walter, T., 2003, 'Historical and cultural variants on the good death', *British Medical Journal*, 327, pp. 218–20.

Wells, S., 2011, *Be Not Afraid: Facing Fear With Faith*, Grand Rapids, MI: Brazos Press.

Weston Area Health NHS Trust, 2020, 'Judaism', *NHS Weston Area Health*, https://www.waht.nhs.uk/en-GB/Our-Services1/Non-Clinical-Services1/Chapel/Faith-and-Culture/Judaism/ (accessed 20.07.2020).

Worden, J. William, 2009, *Grief Counseling and Grief Therapy: A Handbook for the Mental Health Practitioner*, 4th edn, New York: Springer.

Wright, N. T., 2007, *Surprised by Hope*, London: SPCK.

Zimmerman, C. and Rodin, G., 2004, 'The denial of death thesis: sociological critique and implications for palliative care', *Palliative Medicine*, 18 (2), pp. 121–8.